D0484579

Make Every Girl Want You

Everything from Picking-Up Girls to Having a Successful Relationship

John Fate & Steve Reil

Edited by
Craig Coolahan

Please e-mail us at:
menofccr@menofccr.com

axcione publishing
Arlington VA

© 2003 Eric Powders & Gavin Milner. Printed and bound in the United States of America. All rights reserved. No part of this book may be reproduced or transmitted in any form, or by any means, electronic or mechanical, including photocopying, recording, or by an information storage and retrieval system—except by a reviewer who may quote brief passages in a review to be printed in a magazine, newspaper, or on the Web—without permission in writing from the publisher. For more information, please see www.axcione.com.

Visit our website at www.menofccr.com
Contact us at menofccr@menofccr.com

Visit Axcione Publishing website at www.axcione.com

Although the authors and publisher have made every effort to ensure the accuracy and completeness of information contained in this book, we assume no responsibility for errors, inaccuracies, omissions, or any inconsistency herein. Any slights of people, places, or organizations are unintentional.

First printing 2003

ISBN   0-9720166-1-9

LCCN   2003102279

Library of Congress Cataloging-in-Publication Data
Make every girl want you: everything from picking-up girls to having a successful relationship / John Fate, Steve Reil.
P.cm.
ISBN: 0972016619

ATTENTION CORPORATIONS, UNIVERSITIES, COLLEGES, AND PROFESSIONAL ORGANIZATIONS: Quantity discounts are available on bulk purchases of this book for educational or gift purposes, or as premiums for increasing magazine subscriptions or renewals. Special books or book excerpts can also be created to fit specific needs. For information, please contact Axcione Publishing at www.axcione.com

CONTENTS

Dedication
Acknowledgments
Warning—Disclaimer

To Oscar

ACKNOWLEDGMENTS

Editors: *Craig Coolahan, J.L. Goldsworthy, David Moormann*
Edited for Grammar & Punctuation: *James Pennington*
Cover Design: *Lea Psachie, Robert Casillas*
Cover Layout: *Lea Psachie, Robert Casillas*
Cover Photograph: *Juan Chavez*
Cover Model: *Ivykristine Salem*

We would also like to thank: Adrienne, Aicirt, Alex R., Allen, Anand, Andrew, BL, Bex, Blair, Carrie (Tiger), Chris R., Cindy, Claire (Killer), Coke Can, Danielle, Dave P., David S., Elena, Fahd, Fobes, Goldstein, Greenberg, Heather, Hunt, Jason, Jayne, Jess, Jill, K-Brad, Kastler, Kate, Kathy, Kendall, Kinneberg, Kramer, Kristen, Kym, Lacye & Kevin, Lentine, Little Mac, Lori, C. Mahoney, Mary, Matt A, Matt S, Margaret, Meghan, Michele, Mientkiewicz, Misner, Moelchert, Moses, Motts, Nance, Natalie, Nicole C, Nicole P, Nghiem, Oz, Patrick, Pomroy, Quad, Russell, Silverman, Sprinks, Steph, Stoney, Tata-Girl, Thiri, Trish, Troemms, Val, and Van Houten.

And a big thanks to the following friends for putting up with us long before we knew CCR: Ali, Autumn & Stu, Baco & Dedle, BK, Blue & Jenny, The Cavallis, Chiste, Christian, Christine & Guillermo, Colin & Laura, Crowder, Daphne & Will, Darookey, The Deafenbaughs, The Del Pianos, Denise, The Dirties, Doshi, The Eskins & Van Ormans, The Gils & Keatings, Glenn, Gobbo, Goodrich, Greto, Harper, Horgan & Michelle, Hymie & Laura, Jarandeh & Alison, Jeanine & Ken, Jen & Pat, Jennie B, Juice, Julia, K-May, Kant & Marcy, The Entire Kant Family, Kristen, Lee Anne, MacFarland, B. Mahoney, Merkle, Phil & Ingrid, Richard & Meg, Rizzo, Sed, Shamas, The Shoafs, The Simpsons, Stoney & Heather, Tals, Tim & Amy, The Wilsons, Yellowbird, and Zetti.

Thanks to all those who voted on the cover design and who have told their friends about this book.

We would especially like to thank our parents and our families, for all you've taught us about relationships.

– John Fate & Steve Reil

WARNING—DISCLAIMER

This book is designed to provide information on meeting girls and making them want you. It is sold with the understanding that the publisher and authors are not engaged in rendering counseling or other professional services. If expert assistance is required, the services of a competent professional should be sought.

It is not the purpose of this manual to offer all-inclusive information on this topic, but rather to start you off on a path toward forming great relationships with women. You are urged to read all the available material, learn as much as possible about the subject, and tailor the information to your individual needs.

The techniques in this book are not a scheme designed to get sex. Anyone who decides to implement these techniques must expect to invest a lot of time and patience into it. The techniques in this book are powerful, and many have used them with great success. As you implement these techniques, be sure to practice safe sex and use contraceptives.

Every effort has been made to make this manual as complete and as accurate as possible (although the names of all characters referenced in the book have been changed). However, there may be mistakes, both typographical and in content. Therefore, this text should be used only as a general guide and not as the ultimate authority on meeting women and making them want you.

The purpose of this book is to educate and entertain. The authors and Axcione Publishing shall have neither liability nor responsibility to any person or entity with respect to any loss or damage caused (including but not limited to emotional damage), or alleged to have been caused, directly or indirectly, by the information contained in this book.

If you do not wish to be bound by the preceding, you may return this book to the publisher for a full refund.

Chapter 1 – A Need to Improve

We were just a couple of average guys. Neither of us is famous nor plays in a band, but we do have college degrees and professional jobs where we make decent money, nothing to give us status mind you. But despite having what some might consider a lot going for us, including the fact that we're decent looking, we weren't getting any women. Sure, we'd meet women; even get a phone number or two. Sometimes it would actually be the right number and she'd agree to a date. One of these women might even turn into a girlfriend. But when this short-term flame burned its course, it was back to trying our luck again.

Trying our luck. Rolling the dice. This was the problem. This was what bothered us so much about finding women: how much connecting with women could be attributed to luck. There was no logic behind why the occasional woman was interested in us, and as logical people we knew there had to be more than chance at work.

What we recognized, as do all males, was that 10% of the guys seem to get 90% of the women. And those 10% on top seemed to fall into 1 of 3 categories:

1. Really good-looking guys
2. Rich guys
3. Famous guys (including local celebrities)

Simple mathematics told us that guys in these categories couldn't have 90% of the women all at once. So, there's always going to be available women. But plenty of available women or not, we still didn't have the attributes of the guys who get all the women in the first place, anyway.

There was someone, though, who really perplexed us: our friend Oscar. We all know a guy like him. Oscar didn't really stand out for anything, and he wasn't even close to being in one of the three stud categories; yet women *LOVE* Oscar. He has an endless number of beautiful female friends and sleeps with many of them. Every girl who knows him wants him.

On Super Bowl Sunday a few years ago, one of us had lunch with a beautiful female co-worker, Kathryn. At one point, Oscar came up in conversation.

Kathryn: "You saw Oscar? I *LOVE* Oscar. How's he doing?"

John: "Good. Let me ask you something. What the hell is it about Oscar? Every girl I know loves Oscar. I don't get it. What is it about him? He's not that great. He sucks at every sport and he drives that crappy truck."

Kathryn: "Honestly, John. You've just answered your own question."

John: "What does that mean?"

Kathryn: "Listen to you. Everything you say is negative. 'What the hell is it; he sucks....' That's the way you approach everything. Even with me. You're always trying to get attention, cracking jokes. Always insisting that you're heard, but never listening."

John: "What are you talking about?"
Kathryn: "All guys are the same, whether they're rich or good-looking. They're self-absorbed sex fiends. Oscar isn't like that at all. He takes the time to make me feel good about myself, not just boost his own ego. Like last week when I was having a bad day at work, I saw Oscar that evening and he sat and listened to me, asked me questions like he was interested. He reassured me that I was doing a good job at work and that things would turn around."
John: "You've slept with him, haven't you?"
Kathryn: "John! ...Yes."

Based on this conversation, and being fed up with the status quo, we committed ourselves to spending the next year studying Oscar: taking notes on how he moved, how he behaved, how he spoke and how he listened.

We simultaneously committed ourselves to becoming friends with a multitude of women. We would go out with these girls, and watch other guys try to pick them up, some successfully and many unsuccessfully. A year of study resulted in us uncovering three invaluable articles of knowledge for success with women: how girls want to be picked-up, what they're expecting on a first date, and how they want to be treated in a relationship—any relationship.

Armed with this information, we started implementing everything that we had observed and learned. And to our amazement, a fourth guy-who-gets-women category was born: Man of CCR.

Women began responding to us, talking about us, loving us the way they *LOVE* Oscar. And it wasn't difficult. Most of it is obvious once you sit down and consider why it works. The rest of this book explains to you exactly how to be in this fourth category. We can't teach you to be good-looking, rich, or famous, but we can teach you exactly how to be a *Man of CCR*.

Whether you use the information in this book for a serious or casual relationship is up to you. The bottom line is that these techniques will make you a lot more attractive to women.

Of course, we can't alter circumstance, like whether a girl will be single when you meet her. But this book can alter 2 things:

1. You will meet more women
2. More of these women will really want you

But first, a suggestion before getting too involved in this book and the world of CCR: look for a male friend to start with simultaneously. There are several reasons for this:

- You'll want someone to share stories with, compare notes with, and celebrate with
- You'll want someone to discuss issues with and ask questions of
- You can root each other on and build up each other's confidence

You should probably also read Chapter 9, "Coping with Life as a Man of CCR", before you begin. This will enlighten you to what life will be like once you have mastered our techniques.

After we had mastered these techniques ourselves, we decided that we had to write a book to share what we had learned with guys everywhere. One year ago, this book was published. It has been an incredible year. Since then, we have appeared on dozens of radio and TV shows, and have been the subject of numerous articles. We have also been invited to teach courses on a monthly basis in both New York City and San Francisco.

Most importantly to us, however, is that we have received hundreds of responses from you. From the men and women who have read the book or taken our courses, and still have questions. We have since revised the book to better answer the questions that you've been asking us. This updated version of the book was written with that in mind. It incorporates improvements based on all of the feedback we've received from you, the future Men of CCR.

We have also received hundreds of testimonials, both from men and women, thanking us. From men thanking us for helping them learn how to pick up women, to women thanking us for saving their marriages. We wanted to share with you the testimonials of Robert, Michael, Lisa, Corey, Roger, and Julia in particular. To illustrate how this book has helped them, and how it can help you.

From Robert, a 34-year-old man who has been married for eight years:

> "Our marriage had reached the point where we'd only had sex 3 times in the last 5 years. I wasn't even sure if she still loved me anymore.
> I tried a million things, bringing her flowers, taking her out to nice dinners, buying her jewelry. Still nothing. I couldn't even get her to talk about what was wrong with our marriage. Then, a friend of mine got me your book on a whim. He said, 'Hey, Robert. Try reading this. It might help.'
> And it did, CCR has changed my life!
> Not only is our sex life improved, but I feel like, for the first time in about 5 or 6 years, my wife and I actually understand each other. And we enjoy spending time together once again. Thanks John & Steve for saving my marriage."

From Michael, a 19-year-old college student:

> "I've never had much luck with girls. In fact, as much as it hurts me to write this, I made

it to 19 as a virgin. Don't get me wrong, I've been out on dates. But I guess the problem is that I can never get to the 3rd date, if you know what I mean. I just really had no clue how to behave on a date. I read your book cover to cover, and then went back and read it a 2nd time.

A week later, I was sitting next to this really hot girl in my chemistry class. I struck up a conversation, exactly as you guys instructed. That weekend, I found myself having sushi with her. Only this date was different. It was unlike any date I've ever been on. I could tell that she was actually digging me! I don't think she looked at her watch once the entire time.

Best thing is, I didn't even need a 3rd date, because 3 nights later we went out again and she had sex with me! Thank you. Thank you. Thank you."

From Lisa, a single gal who withheld her age:

"I bought a copy for my friend, Harold. Harold's a great guy. I've been friends with him for 8 years, and let me just say that he has not had much success with the ladies. Which really isn't fair, because he's the world's sweetest guy. Of course, as a woman, I can kind of understand why he doesn't have success with women. But the thing is, as much as I've tried to explain it to him, he just doesn't get it.

So I heard you guys on a radio show, and decided to buy your book for him. You guys said in 150 pages what I haven't been able to get Harold to understand in 8 years! Harold just has so much more confidence now. I can tell when I'm around him that he actually, finally, feels comfortable interacting with women. Sure, he's not a walking, talking babe magnet, but he's so much better off.

In fact, I recently introduced him to a couple of my female friends, who have both since asked about him. I mean, *my* friends – asking about Harold? That just doesn't happen! I'm almost starting to get jealous! Thanks guys, for a great book. I think every girl should buy it for her platonic male friends!"

From Corey, a 25-year-old professional:

"It's been a few years since I graduated from college. I have a good job and live in the city now, but man it's so much tougher to meet women than it was in college. In college, there were girls over at the frat house all the time. It was so easy to hook-up. Now, I can't even figure out where to meet women, let alone hook-up.

I ordered your book, and read it cover to cover in an hour. I discovered that my main problem is that I was looking for girls in all of the wrong places. Great book, guys— thanks a ton. I've already told all of my friends about it."

From Roger, who is 37 years old and divorced:

"I finally understand why my first marriage failed. And let me tell you, until now I was clueless. I read your guys' book, because I'm single now. And I really read it for tips on where to meet women. But what really helped me is that you pointed out every single thing I did wrong in my first marriage.

I'm dating someone now, and I definitely want to get married again someday. I don't know if it'll be to her, but I feel like I finally know what it will take to make a marriage work. I would recommend your book to any guy who wants to make his second marriage work."

From Julia, who is married—happily now—and requested that we not print her age:

"I've been trying for years to get Bill to read 'relationship books.' But I haven't been able to get him to read a damn one. I saw you guys on TV, and figured—what the hell—I'll get your book, basically as a last resort. I gave it to Bill, and he read the entire thing that night.

Afterward, he came up to me, gave me a big hug, and said: 'Honey, I have 2 things to tell you. #1: I want you to know how beautiful you are. And #2: I'm sorry I haven't told you that in 13 years.'"

There are two essential elements illustrated by these testimonials. The first is that the book helped each one of these individuals in a different way. The second is that the book was successful for them because it helped break down preconceived notions and old stereotypes that were impeding their success with the opposite sex.

Over and over again, we are amazed to find that although we receive many of the same questions from readers—as you will read later in the book—what they take away from the book is a very individual thing. And the reason for this is simple: we all focus our attention on different things.

For example, when we started studying Oscar, we'd see him do something and say to ourselves, 'Hey, I do that. Why don't I get all the women he does?' But then the next day he'd do something we would have never done, and we'd realized that the whole was certainly greater than the sum of its parts in this case.

In other words, we're all doing some of the right things, just not all of the right things, because for whatever reason one aspect of dating holds more importance to us over the other. And ultimately we spend so much time concentrating on this that we can't let go and expand our line of thinking. What is clear is that we need to expand our way of looking at dating and relationships, and attempt to arm ourselves with the entire package. The CCR package.

What we also realized was that not only do you need the whole package, but you also need to break down many of your preconceived notions about what women want.

For example, women don't want jerks. They want guys who are compassionate and provide them with reassurance. Women don't want expensive presents and fancy dinners; they want intimacy and understanding.

When we were studying Oscar we kept saying to ourselves, 'I can't believe he's using that approach; he's going to fail for sure.' But he would always prove us wrong, and he succeeded in showing us the right way. And with this book, we think that we can pass this knowledge on to you, as we have to so many already.

Let's move on and examine what precisely we mean by CCR.

Chapter 2 – What Is CCR?

CCR is based on the fact that the needs of men and women are inherently different. Guys are simple— we want attractive women. Of course personality and intelligence matter, but a woman has to have, at least a little, some conventional beauty; otherwise, a good personality is really irrelevant.

Appearance matters to women as well, but not nearly as much. The reason that we were originally so pathetic is that we approached things from a guy's perspective. We noticed that a lot of cocky, arrogant guys seemed to be successful with women. We copied their obnoxious behavior, yet it didn't work for us. Why? Because it's a myth that women like guys who are jerks. And here's where and how this myth originated. Back in high school and college, about 10% of the guys realized that because they either played on a sports team, were in a popular fraternity, or were really good-looking, they got a lot of girls. What ended up happening is that this 10% got so many girls that they naturally became arrogant and cocky.

As we got older, new guys joined the ranks of the 10% by becoming rich or famous, or finally growing into their looks, and they too became arrogant, cocky jerks because of all the women they were getting.

What this looks like to the remaining 90% of the male population is that these guys get women because they're jerks. That's simply not the case. The truth is that these guys are arrogant jerks because they get so many women as a result of having one or more of the attributes of the "ten percenters." Acting like a jerk for the sole purpose of attracting more women simply won't work if you're not in the 10%.

We ran an experiment to prove this point. We took seven of our closest male friends and made a pact. For two straight weeks, we went around trying to pick up women acting like complete jerks. We all failed miserably. Not one of us picked up a girl in ten nights of trying.

Conclusion: you can't get girls by being a jerk. If you already get girls because you're the star quarterback, rich or connected, then you can get away with it. If, however, you're not in the top 10%, and odds suggest that you're not, then being a jerk to women will ensure that you remain a lonely, lonely man. The bottom line is that women do not like jerks because they're jerks; women like these guys because they have something else going for them.

It wasn't until we started looking at things from a female's perspective that we became successful. Let's face it, women's lives are much tougher than men's, and this goes much deeper than their monthly visitor and not having upper body strength. For instance, almost 15% of girls (or 1 in 7) have been the victim of rape or sexual assault by age 25.[1] Look around you, at the women in your office or in your classes. Statistically, at least one has been a victim. It's a disturbing reality.

In addition to acts of violence, approximately 40% of girls have become pregnant by age 20,[2] and 18% of them have had either an abortion or a miscarriage.[3] Again, look around you. One out of every 6 or 7 girls you see has either been raped, been sexually assaulted, had an abortion, or had a miscarriage.

Other startling statistics include the fact that by age 20[4], up to 3.2% of girls are anorexic, and up to 3.6% of girls are bulimic[5]. Now there are probably some women reading this that are shocked that we included these statistics. And you're probably thinking, "You're quoting these statistics in a book on helping guys pick women up?" Although this seems crass at first, there are 2 points that we really want to hit home with guys by doing this.

First, guys don't realize what a high percentage of women are affected by these problems. We don't realize that many of the women that we see on a daily basis have been raped or sexually assaulted, have had an abortion or a miscarriage, or are bulimic or anorexic.

The second point we want to make is that as guys we *really* don't understand the impact that these things have on women. Our good friend Carrie has tearfully relayed to us on multiple occasions the trauma of having had an abortion:

> "It's been ten years since the abortion, and not a day goes by that I don't think about it. I'm still not sure it was the right decision. Sure, I was young, but I could've made things work. My little girl would be 10 years old today."

As you can see, these problems have long-lasting effects on a woman's life. Women have it tough, and men rarely acknowledge this. In fact, we contribute a fair amount to making things difficult for women. Like the way that we'll say anything to get a woman in bed and construct elaborate lies as to why we're breaking up with them.

Bottom line: Be glad that you're a guy. Not only because we don't have to deal with many of the issues previously mentioned, but also because we don't have to deal with women deliberately making our lives worse than they have to be, like we do to them. For example, when men rate the most important traits they look for in women, beauty often shows up #1. On the other hand, when women rate the most important traits they look for in a man, looks usually are much lower on the list. In other words, it doesn't matter how ugly, poor or dumb you are; it won't stop you from getting women, at least not for these reasons. But you still have to know what women want.

So, what do women ultimately want? Like we said, we as guys really want physically attractive women. We're simple. Women, on the other hand, want someone they can connect with.

So now you're thinking, "What in the world does that mean? How do you make a connection?" It's really a two-step process. The first step is creating an initial attraction, so she'll go out with you. After all, how can the two of you connect if she won't even give you the time of day? The second step is actually making the connection.

So how do you make yourself more attractive to women, so they'll at least give you a chance? Unlike with men, it has very little to do with physical attraction. Attraction for a woman is much more complex than it is for a guy. Let's be honest, when we say that a girl is hot, we mean that she's got long blond hair, blue eyes, and huge cans.

For women, there are many components. This is evidenced in how women now respond to us. Back in our pathetic days, no girl would ever call us hot, because we're not. We're just average looking. Nowadays, though, girls tell us that we're hot on a regular basis. Why? It's not because we've improved our physical appearance. We haven't had gym memberships since college.

It's because we know that it's not physical attraction alone that makes a woman fall for a guy, but a complex combination of things, such as how a guy makes her feel about herself, how well he listens to her, and whether she thinks he views her purely as a sex object, to name a few.

As mentioned, we will never be rich, famous, or good-looking; luckily, however, we've figured out that by focusing on other aspects of attraction, women actually consider us hot!

You see this play out in Hollywood all the time. A male actor, who really isn't all that good looking, gets cast in a romantic comedy and suddenly women everywhere think he's so hot. Yet if they met this same guy walking down the street they wouldn't give him a second thought. To illustrate this, we asked our good friend Suzanne what she thinks of Adam Sandler:

> "Oh my God, Adam Sandler is SO hot! You don't understand—he is SO hot! In *Big Daddy*, the way he interacts with little Julian is so cute! I just wish I could be Layla in that movie!"

We next asked Suzanne what she thinks of our friend Jason, who is constantly told that he looks exactly like Adam Sandler:

> "You mean what do I think of how he looks? I guess he's OK, pretty much average looking. If I saw him on the street, he wouldn't really turn my head. I don't know. I guess there are some girls who might find him attractive, but I don't really go for that look. You're not gonna tell him I said this are you?"

We were so intrigued by this experiment, that we wanted to try it again. This time, we decided to ask girls what they thought of our friend Mark, and what they thought of our friend Brian. Mark and Brian are identical twins. To this day, we still have trouble telling them apart. Their personalities, however, are quite distinct. Mark is a natural Man of CCR: extremely complimentary of women, and a great listener. He's the type of guy who makes everyone around him feel great. Brian, however, is loud, boisterous, and borders on being obnoxious. He is always trying to be the center of attention. We first asked our friend Erin about Mark:

> "Mark's *such* a great guy! As you guys know, I've had a crush on him for like 3 years. But we're just friends, and I'm cool with that. I just love being around him. I know that whenever I'm in a bad mood, I can spend time with Mark, and I'll always end up in a great mood!"

We then asked Erin about Brian:

> "Um, Brian's OK. You know. I've been really good friends with Mark for years, and so Brian's often there when we hang out. And he's OK. He's a nice guy. He means well. I mean, he's a little immature, but I'm sure he'll grow out of that someday. And then he'll probably have more success with the ladies!"

So, as previously stated, the first step in the dating game is getting the girl to go out with you. To give you a chance. To make her say to herself, "You know, this guy isn't rich, isn't famous, and isn't particularly handsome, but I really enjoy being with him. I like the way he makes me feel."

So how do you make a girl want you? How do you make a girl attracted to you so that she'll want to go out with you? The first step is to show her that *you* like who *she* is as a person and, in turn, make *her* like *herself*. As mentioned, women have a lot of problems that men never consider. Many women aren't happy with themselves; they have low self-esteem and tend to have quite a few insecurities about themselves.

Ask any woman if there's anything she'd like to change about herself, and she can probably rattle off a list of 20 things. A friend of ours, Candace, an absolute drop-dead knock-out, had this to say about herself:

> "Yeah, I need to lose a little weight. I've also always wanted to be 4 inches taller. I'd like to have a smoother complexion, and darker skin tone. I wish I had longer eyelashes, and bigger breasts. There's a lot of things I'd like to change about myself."

If you're like us, you're probably thinking to yourself, "Wow, this sounds really unhealthy." Yes, it actually is. And modern culture, particularly Western society, is to blame.

The images and standards of beauty conveyed to women through the media is the primary culprit. But it's not our purpose to discuss modern society and its effect on women's self-image. Just pointing out the correlation is enough for our purposes.

Showing a woman that you like who she is, and in turn making her like herself, is huge. If you can be that rare guy who does this, then women everywhere will want to be around you. This is why women love Oscar. When you first see Oscar, there's nothing about him that makes him immediately appealing. He's not rich, not famous, and not good-looking.

Once you get into a conversation with Oscar, however, everyone (guys and girls) thinks, "Wow! What a great guy! He's complimentary and really interested in me as a person. I just feel so good when I'm around him." Oscar just has a way of making everyone around him feel better about themselves. For average guys, tapping into this knowledge about attraction is gold, and the key to your success with women. This will put you on par with all of those rich, famous, and good-looking guys out there.

We'd like to make one final point before we get into the discussion on how to make yourself more attractive to women: This is NOT about one-night stands. Honestly, we're not good-looking enough for that. If you look at most of the guys having one-night stands, they're rich, famous, or good-looking. If you're in one of those three categories, it's very easy to walk into a bar, project such status, and take a woman home.

Projecting attractiveness in the manner we use is much more difficult; do not expect to be able to take a woman home the night you meet her. With your newfound knowledge, however, you *can* intrigue her enough by your personality that she'll go out on a date with you, so that you can continue to show her what an incredible guy you are.

If you bought this book looking for tips on one-night stands, then we sincerely apologize and encourage you to return the book; we will gladly refund your money. If, however, you're like us, and you've come to terms with the fact that you're not rich, famous, or good-looking, then read on. We've got a lot to share with you.

Compliments

So what does CCR stand for? CCR is the most important acronym you will ever learn in the quest for women, and it stands for Compliments, Compassion and Reassurance. Giving compliments is the first method in making a girl want you. Women love compliments; it makes them feel good about themselves. But for some reason most guys don't compliment women. If they knew how women would reciprocate when receiving compliments, they would certainly go out of their way to start.

What should you compliment women on? Just about anything: their necklace, perfume, eyes, shoes, watch, bracelet, hat, scarf, hair, the color of their shirt.

Women spend a lot of time "accessorizing", and love it when you notice the things they've done. As long as you do it sincerely, they'll love you for it. Try it in your daily interactions. Don't go overboard, but try to pay one compliment to every woman you interact with this week. Say it sincerely, and do it with a smile.

Here's an example of our friend Jeanine talking about one of our students, Doug, a Man of CCR:

> "I love being around Doug. He's so complimentary of me, and makes me feel so good about myself. Just last week I was wearing a new ring that my parents had given me for Christmas, and Doug noticed it immediately and told me how beautiful it is. Why wouldn't I want to be around Doug?"

If you observe two girls talking to each other, you will hear a stream of compliments:

"Oh, I love those shoes!"
"That's such a pretty necklace!"
"Where'd you get that top from?"

Why do women compliment each other so much? Because they love to receive compliments. A compliment can brighten up a woman's day like you wouldn't imagine. Are we telling you to go around and start making up compliments? Absolutely not. What we're saying is that if there's a girl who you're interested in, then there must be a few things that you like about her. So don't be afraid to tell her about these things. You will be shocked at how it makes her day.

Don't confine your compliments simply to physical traits either. A girl will want to know that you like her for more than just her physical attributes. If a girl dabbles in art, for example, and you like some of her paintings, be sure to tell her. Observe Mike in this example:

27

> Mike, upon entering Daphne's apartment: "Wow, I really like the decorating. These paintings are amazing!"
> Daphne: "Thanks. I painted them."
> Mike: "Are you serious?"
> Daphne: "Yep."
> Mike: "Wow! You are an incredible artist. You're really talented."
> Daphne: "Thanks."
> Mike: "I really like the way you painted that meadow in this one. It could be a Van Gogh."

As we talk about later in this chapter, be sure to only compliment a woman if you sincerely mean it. Women can see right through insincere compliments.

Once you're in a relationship, don't forget to keep up the compliments. It is important in a relationship to move on to deeper, more meaningful compliments that show how much you care for her:

> "Carrie, I just wanted to tell you that you are an absolutely amazing person. I have so much fun when I'm around you. I'm glad that we've gotten to be so close."
> "Dana, you are one of the most incredible people I have ever met."

Another important category of compliments is *Third-Party Compliments*. This means complimenting people who are not present. Most of the time when you hear two people talking about someone else, they're saying negative things about that person. Women will be extremely impressed and appreciate the fact that you not only don't say derogatory things about people behind their backs, but instead have positive things to say about them. What's more, these women will then start imagining all of the wonderful things you're saying about them when they're not around.

The most effective method by which to do this is simply to state how great someone is when his or her name comes up in conversation:

Rachel: "I ran into Suzanne the other day."
Doug: "She's awesome. I've been dying to see her. It's been so long and she's such a blast to hang out with."
Rachel: "Yeah, I saw her in the grocery store."
Doug: "How's she doing?"
Rachel: "She just broke up with her boyfriend, but she seems to be taking it well."
Doug: "That's too bad. I hope she's doing okay."

A final comment about compliments: don't ever offer a compliment that can be misconstrued. If the context is questionable, it's better to withhold. There are plenty of other things to compliment. An example would be a girl with big breasts dressed in a tight, low-cut top. Don't ever tell her that you really like her shirt. Our friend Susan, who has large breasts, had this to say about compliments:

"I love guys who compliment me, but not on cheesy or stupid things. And I hate it when guys look at my breasts or compliment my breasts. I really like wearing low-cut tops that show them off, but don't tell me you like the shirt when you really mean that you like my breasts. That's such a turn-off."

An acceptable compliment, on the other hand, is:

"I like the color of your shirt, Rachel. It really brings out the green in your eyes."

You'll get bonus points for being observant of Rachel's eye color.

Compassion

The second C, Compassion, is the next key ingredient to making a girl want you. Your current response to a woman telling you her problems might be something along the lines of contemplating suicide. The only reason you were listening in the first place was likely because she's a gorgeous girl. You would never listen to an ugly girl complain. While this reaction to listening to a beautiful woman's problems is nothing more than male instinct, it's time to change your behavior. No, not by listening to an ugly girl, but by actually enjoying listening to all girls.

The next time a woman discusses her problems with you, don't just act like you're listening, but genuinely listen. Listen to every word she says. Ask her questions to demonstrate your interest. And, more importantly, match her emotion.

Emotion matching is really the key to compassion. By matching a woman's mood, whether happy or sad, she feels emotionally connected to you. If a woman is telling a sad story, respond with:

"Awww, I'm really sorry to hear that."

If a woman is complaining about something, show that you understand:

"Yeah, I know what you mean."

If a woman is telling a happy story, get happy with her:

"Wow! That's incredible! What did you do?"

A key difference between men and women is a want of resolution. When men have a problem, they want to find the root cause and resolve it. Women don't want to solve their problems; all they want to do is to clear the air and get the problem off of their chest. So, when a girl is talking to you about a problem, don't try to solve it. Just listen to her. Ask her more questions to draw out the problem, but don't offer solutions. Guaranteed, you'll be better off by offering her your ear than your wisdom. Here's how to handle the situation:

> Carrie: "Things haven't been going well at my job lately."
>
> Doug: "Why?"
>
> Carrie: "We're about to go through a round of layoffs, and I think that my job's gonna be one of the cuts."
>
> Doug: "Why do you think that?"
>
> Carrie: "Well, the project that I've spent the last 6 months working on was just cut from the budget, and now I don't have anything to work on."
>
> Doug: "That's too bad. Sorry to hear that, but it would be their loss. You're so talented you won't have any problem finding a new job. You'll probably find a better job. If it happens, it's a blessing in disguise."
>
> Carrie: "Really? You think so?"
>
> Doug: "Absolutely! Your skill set is in such high demand, and you're so good at what you do. You won't have any problem finding another job."
>
> Carrie: "Thanks, Doug. You know, I really love talking to you. I always feel so much better."

When a girl talks to you about her boyfriend problems, just listen to her. Most guys who listen to a girl talk about her boyfriend problems encourage her to break-up with him. How many times have you heard a guy make the following snide remarks?

> "You can do better than him."
> "You should be with me, not him."

"Why do you put up with that? I'd treat you so much better than that."

These comments only serve to frustrate women. It shows a lack of compassion and turns women away from the guy who's saying it. Instead, help her to see the positives in the situation. Point out the good traits about the guy. Reassure her that only someone in love talks that way about someone else. Tell her things will work out. Our friend Karen had this to say about guys listening to her:

> "I love it when a guy listens to me. I don't mean acting like he's listening, but really listening. It's easy to tell, because he looks me in the eyes and not around the room. I really hate it when I'm talking about my relationship with Daniel and a guy tells me that I should break-up with him or that I can do better. I mean, I know we've gone through some bad times, and I know we fight and stuff, but I love him. I'm not gonna break-up with Daniel to be with some slimy rebound hound."

There's a good possibility that things won't work out with her boyfriend anyway, and if you're there listening to her and showing compassion, there's a good chance you'll be dating her next.

Here's an example of the type of approach to take. Jake had met Sherrie 3 weeks ago, and they had been e-mailing and chatting at work frequently:

> Jake: "So how are things going with you and Mark?"
> Sherrie: "Not too well."
> Jake: "Why not?"
> Sherrie: "Well, you know, it's a long-distance relationship. And the last few times we've

talked on the phone we've had stupid
fights over nothing."

Jake: "I'm sorry to hear that."

Sherrie: "It's just getting really difficult to keep
things going long distance."

Jake: "You know, Sherrie, I hear the way you
talk about Mark. I know how much you
love him, and I know how important he is
to you. I'm sure things will work out."

When a woman is talking to you about her
feelings, *never* imply that her feelings are wrong.
Validate her feelings. Tell her that she has a right to feel
that way. A friend of ours, Lisa, had this to say about
her boyfriend, who doesn't respect her feelings:

"I was telling my boyfriend the other day how I
felt sad about my friend losing her job.
And he told me that I shouldn't be upset;
it wasn't me losing my job. I mean, how
can my feelings be wrong? They're my
feelings. I can't control them. And feelings
can't be wrong."

When a girl feels sad or depressed, you may
think that it is because of the most ridiculous thing
that you've ever heard. But don't dare tell her that. Just
validate her feelings.

Reassurance

The R in CCR, Reassurance, goes hand in hand
with compassion. An excellent time to provide
reassurance is when a woman is discussing her
problems. And if she is, then your first order of
business is to provide compassion. But somewhere in
the discussion, be sure to reassure her that everything
is okay and that things will get better.

Sure, it sounds stupid to guys. We don't need reassurance; we know that things will improve. Reassurance, however, goes a long way with women.

How many times has a woman asked you to choose, out of 5 different outfits, what she'll wear that evening? Then, after getting dressed, she asks you if you think she picked the right outfit. Don't get angry with her for constantly asking you the same questions. Simply reassure her and she will love you.

This is one of the major points of contention between men and women in relationships. Women drive men absolutely insane with their constant need for reassurance:

"Do I look fat?"
"Does this dress look good on me?"
"Should I order the chicken or the steak?"

Don't let it bother you. Just accept the fact that this is how women are, and you will be miles ahead of any other guy. A friend of ours, Suzanne, had this to say about her need for reassurance:

"I know it sounds stupid, but I need approval on my choices. I mean, I need to know that my friends like my boyfriend and stuff. And when I go shopping, I always bring a friend with me because I need to hear someone else say that a dress looks good on me. I know it sounds stupid, but it just makes me feel better."

Now take it a step further and enjoy the fact that women need reassurance. You will be one of the few guys who will not only provide reassurance, but also enjoy it. Look forward to women asking your advice, because it will give you another chance to show them what a great guy you are. This will, in turn, make them want you.

Not Being a Doormat

There is a key difference between being a Man of CCR and a doormat. This difference is being able to convey to women that your life does not revolve around them. If you come running every time a girl calls, then she will realize that she can walk all over you. When we teach CCR in our courses, we often hear this complaint:

> "I've been the doormat. I've tried CCR. I've been the guy who she walks all over. The guy who listens to a girl's problems. But women always view me as a friend. I always end up as the doormat."

After talking to these guys for a few minutes, we inevitably discover that they have no life outside of the woman with whom they're obsessed. Whenever she calls, they're always sitting at home, ready to talk, as if they were waiting for her to call.

Successful Men of CCR are busy with their own lives, and while happy to spend time with women, are not always available due to prior commitments. Dwelling on one particular girl, and relying on her for your happiness in life—before you're actually in a relationship—is deadly. Once you're in a relationship, it is OK to plan your life with someone else in mind (hey, that's what marriage is all about), but doing this too soon is a huge turn-off to women.

Suppose you ask a woman out, and she asks what night works for you. Look at the difference between these two responses:

> "Oh, any night next week works. All I really do is sit at home and watch TV most nights anyway."

> "Wednesday night works best for me. I could actually go out Tuesday evening, but it would have to be later because I'm playing

racquetball after work. Or we can grab lunch Thursday, but at night I'm grabbing dinner with some friends."

Look at the difference between these two responses. The first response conveys to the woman that you have no life, with is very unattractive to women. A woman would expect that this type of guy would be a doormat whom she could walk all over. The second response, however, shows that you have interests of your own. This is very attractive to women, and shows them that you really are a Man of CCR, and not a doormat.

We've all heard the myth that nice guys can't get girls. This is completely untrue. It is because most "nice guys", even guys who use CCR, don't show these women that they have a life. If a nice guy is using CCR and isn't getting girls, it's because he's dwelling on women, rather than having a life of his own.

We have a friend, Roger, who is witty, good looking, has a great sense of humor, and is very intelligent. Every girl we talked to always said they loved Roger, but that they would never hook-up with him. The reason Roger never had sexual encounters with women is that he was insecure with himself and thus always came running whenever a girl called. Roger never had a life of his own, and all of his female friends knew that whenever they needed a shoulder to cry on, Roger would *always* be there. In fact, a friend of ours, Maryanne, perceived Roger's insecurities as a lack of confidence (more on confidence soon):

"Aw, I love Roger. He's such a great guy. The second you see him it just brightens your day. I just love the way that he always asks me how I'm doing and how I've been. And how he really listens to me. He just always puts me in such a good mood. Everybody likes him. That's why I don't understand why his confidence is so low.

36

He's a great guy and every girlfriend of mine loves being around him. But without confidence, they're not going to want him. I would never think about hooking up with him. His lack of confidence is just really unattractive."

Roger was very successful at CCR. Women loved him and were always around him because he listened to them and cared about them for who they are. But, these women did not *want* him. He practiced CCR, but he wasn't a Man of CCR. This subtle yet distinct difference causes most of us to think that nice guys don't get girls. If these guys could adequately convey to women, however, that they actually have a life, so many women would want them. We have since taught Roger to be a Man of CCR (and he is doing quite well for himself now!).

Sincerity

A point about sincerity now: CCR will fail if you are not sincere in your actions. We are not telling you to go around fabricating compliments and acting like you care about women's problems. What we're telling you is that if you truly like someone, then you should care not only about her good points, but also about helping her through tough situations.

Learn to embrace the fact that women are this way, and learn to love it. At first, you will probably have to force yourself, but once you see the results of your actions you will truly look forward to having women share their problems with you.

You'll know if you're sincere in your compliments, compassion, and reassurance when women start opening up to you. When we were learning CCR, we reached a point at which women whom we had just met started to open up emotionally to us. It was odd, but it was a great sign that we were doing something right.

So make sure all of your compliments, compassion, and reassurance are sincere. Once you become a Man of CCR, you will see just how powerful it is. You can ignore everything in men's magazines about how women really want a guy who can cook or give great massages. With CCR you can get away without opening doors or giving massages. Of course, every little thing helps. But recognize that CCR is on an entirely different level. Women will compromise almost anything else just for CCR. First learn CCR, and then worry about learning how to cook.

We wish you the best of luck on your CCR endeavor. So grab a male confidant to share the adventure. Trust us; it's more than worth it.

If you have any questions about CCR, please e-mail us at menofccr@menofccr.com. We'll be more than happy to help out. We also offer courses (currently in New York City and San Francisco) and one-on-one consultations over the phone; check www.menofccr.com for details.

Chapter 3 – Getting Started: How to Meet Women

You can't use CCR unless you first meet women. So how do you meet women?

When you walk up to a random girl in a bar, walking down the street, or in a bookstore, do you know what the first thing is that usually goes through her mind? It's usually along the lines of "Why is this guy bothering me?"

Women constantly complain that they can't meet the right guy. They all thought they'd be married by whatever age they're currently at. And even though they still aren't, the first thing that often goes through a woman's mind when she meets a marriage prospect is, "Why is this guy bothering me?"

It's important for guys to understand this. So many guys wonder why a girl won't give out her contact info, even though you think you've made a good first impression and the two of you seem to be hitting it off. The fact is, you were probably bothering her. As guys, we don't start off on even ground with women; we start off in negative territory. It's not as simple as making a good impression with a girl; you also have to overcome the fact that she may just not want to talk to a stranger right now.

In particular, the more attractive the girl, the more likely it is that you're not the first guy to come along and interrupt her that day. She's probably been approached on the subway on her way to work, while she was at work, while she was out grabbing lunch, and again on her way home.

With this in mind, we have classified meeting environments into 3 categories: *Naturally-Inviting*, *Moderately-Inviting*, and *Bothersome*. As you would guess, the more naturally inviting an environment is, the more likely a girl will want to talk to you.

So many guys spend all of their time trying to meet women in bothersome environments, not realizing that they're fighting an uphill battle. While it is certainly possible to meet women in any of these three types of environments, we have found that success rates among these environments vary greatly. If you currently spend all of your time trying to meet women at bars, hopefully now you'll try to get invited to a few parties.

Naturally-Inviting Environments

The most natural way to meet a woman is through a mutual friend. This is actually how we meet most of the women whom we date. When women meet a guy through a mutual friend, it is not a bother. If their friend went through the trouble of making the introduction, then they will usually sit there and talk to the guy.

The best friends for this are female friends, because they are more likely to know other females and more likely to introduce you to these friends than are your male friends.

We talk more about getting vouches from your female friends in the chapter "The Power of Friendship."

First, however, read what our friend Sheila had to say about how she prefers to meet guys:

> "I feel so much more comfortable meeting guys either at a friend's party or through a friend. It's not that I'm an especially busy person, but it seems that guys always approach me at the wrong time. But if you're going out to dinner with some friends, and they bring along other friends, that's a good time to meet new people. You're already in a social mood, and you know that because these guys are friends with your friends they must be worth meeting!"

Other than a direct introduction by a mutual friend, the next best way to meet women in an inviting environment is at a party or social gathering. When women go to parties, they expect to meet new people, and are open and receptive to it. So try to get invited to a lot of parties. How? By having a lot of acquaintances.

You don't need to be best friends with people to be invited to their parties; you simply need to be acquaintances. Get to know everyone in your workplace. If you live in an apartment building, get to know other people in your building. Join some clubs or social groups, such as a local softball team or a wine-tasting group. The more acquaintances you have and the more people you know, the more parties you will likely get invited to.

This applies to men of all ages. Whether you're a college kid wanting to get invited to more raging keggers, or in your forties and want to get invited to more backyard cookouts, you'll meet more women either way. Group gatherings like these are the absolute best way to meet women, because they are naturally inviting environments. The women there will be expecting to meet new people, and thus very open to it.

Moderately-Inviting Environments

What if you want to meet women but, for whatever reason, can't go to a lot of parties and don't seem to meet a lot of women through your friends? If you can't seem to meet women at parties, or through your friends, the next best thing to do is to join groups or clubs that participate in moderately-inviting activities.

So what do we mean by groups or clubs that participate in moderately-inviting activities? Here are some examples: a co-ed sports team, an adult education class (such as a cooking or wine-tasting class), the local chapter of your alumni association, or a church or temple. When women are in these environments, their primary purpose often isn't to meet new people. They are usually aware, however, that they will meet new people, and are moderately inviting toward the men who approach them. Our friend Becky had this to say about how she met her current boyfriend in a cooking class:

> "I signed-up for a cooking class, because I've always wanted to be able to cook better. I wasn't looking to meet a guy. But there was this one guy in my class—he's not the world's best-looking guy, but I really enjoyed talking to him. We happened to end up next to each other a few weeks in a row, and finally he asked me out.
>
> Once we went out, I got to see what a great guy he is. He really cared about me as a person. We've been dating for eight months now, and things are going great! I'm so glad I decided to take that cooking class!"

Another moderately-inviting environment is an apartment building. Believe it or not, most women actually enjoy meeting their neighbors. We have met quite a few women just by starting conversations in the parking lot, or while waiting for the elevator. After chatting with a woman a few times, she will often be quite receptive if you stop by her apartment.

The workplace provides an additional moderately-inviting environment. True, women are there to work, not to meet guys. But meeting guys at work is in the back of their head (as meeting girls is with us). Another example is at the gym. This, like the workplace, provides an environment in which you can make small talk repeatedly with the same women to establish some level of comfort. Again, most women don't go to the gym with the intention of meeting a guy, but it is in the back of their head.

The added bonus of joining these groups or clubs is that, as we've previously mentioned, you get to meet a lot of guys who will, in turn, invite you to their parties where there will be women. Now let's take a look at environments that are less inviting.

Bothersome Environments

Although bothersome environments are the most difficult places to get to know women, they're also, ironically, the most common places for men to meet women.

So what are the best bothersome places in which to meet women? Well, there's a long list: bars, bookstores, concerts, subways, buses, restaurants, coffee shops, grocery stores, festivals, parks, walking down the street, basically anywhere.

Despite the abundance of women in these places we've dubbed them bothersome places for a reason: women tend to act like they're being bothered when approached in these places. In fact, they will often be downright cold to you, and most men don't recognize why. At least in inviting environments, if a woman has a boyfriend or isn't feeling well, she will often tell you that up front.

In bothersome environments, there can be a number of reasons why a woman is acting so cold to you. For example, a woman in a grocery store may actually be there to buy groceries. In which case, it is quite possible that she doesn't want to be bothered by anyone right now.

When you approach a woman in a bar, there are numerous reasons why she might not want to talk to you. She may be on a girls' night out, and the group isn't out to meet guys, in which case you're serving as an interruption and a bother.

She may be out to meet up with a specific guy, and he just hasn't arrived yet. She may have a boyfriend. She may have just ended a relationship, and isn't ready to meet anyone. In fact, she may be very bitter toward men right now, and really doesn't want to be "hit on." She may have just started dating someone, and isn't interested in meeting anyone else. Or, maybe she's just not feeling well.

As we touched upon, the real downside of meeting women in these bothersome environments is the lack of explanation you will get from these women as to why they're being cold to you. The problem is that so many guys take this rejection personally. Take this account from our friend Jake, of a guy, Ryan, who didn't need to beat himself up over this one:

> "I was out with those girls from UGA last night grabbing some drinks. After a few minutes, this random guy came up, introduced himself as Ryan, and tried to talk to Sara. Sara, you know, she's got a boyfriend, so she pretty much ignored him. After two minutes of painful persistence, which seemed like an eternity to the guy I'm sure, he finally took the hint and left.
>
> Five minutes later, Sara's boyfriend Mark finally arrived and sat down next to her. Sara immediately looked up, smiled, and

started chatting with him, although they
didn't kiss hello or anything.
I glanced over at that guy Ryan and he was just
so down on himself. He thought Mike was
some random guy with game who
succeeded where he had failed. It was so
sad. I almost went over and filled him in.
But it was kind of funny, too."

If this happens to you, do NOT take it personally.
Do not think that you lack game. In fact, the two of us
usually only go out to bars when we're bringing girls
with us. We rarely try to pick up girls in bars, because
it is such a tough environment. Even though we know
what we're doing, we hate the fact that we don't know
which girls have boyfriends, which girls are on a girls'
night out, and which girls are there to meet guys. And
thus, we primarily stick to meeting girls at social
gatherings, or through some of the social activities we
participate in.

Here's the even bigger problem. Most guys, when
they go out at night, think they can recognize which
women are out to be picked up. How often have you
heard a guy make a comment like:

"Look at the way those two are dressed. They're
definitely looking for some action tonight."

There is no correlation between the way a girl is
dressed and the reason she's out—none at all.

It was so shocking to the two of us when we first
started becoming friends with females, and finally got to
see things from the inside. We've been out with groups
of girls on numerous occasions. It's so much fun
hanging out at the girls' apartments, as they're all
getting ready, and hearing them talk about their plans
for the night.

Take this account from our friend Mike, who
went out one night with a group of girls who all have

boyfriends (they were his Subconscious Vouch; more on that in the Chapter "The Power of Friendship"):

"You guys should've seen these girls—dressed to kill. They all looked so hot, wearing low-cut tops and mini skirts. But listen to how they were talking as they were getting ready and putting on their make-up:

'Oh, look at us—we're gonna get so much attention tonight.'
'Yeah, guys are gonna be coming up to us left and right.'
'I don't think we'll have to pay for a single drink tonight.'
'It's a shame we're all so in love with our boyfriends—oh well, taking the time to get dressed up is worth it for the free drinks!'

Their boyfriends are all in med. school, and had to study that night. Cool group of guys— I've played golf with them. Anyhow, it was so much fun watching guys approach them all night, watching guys try to get with them on the dance floor.
And because of the great vouch I had, I met these two really good-looking med. school girls who are friends with their boyfriends."

It's really unfair to guys, because when guys go out and see this group of girls, we have no clue that they all have boyfriends. So many guys wasted so much time approaching these girls, talking to these girls, and trying to dance with these girls. Yet Mike sat there and laughed at these guys. As good friends of the girls, he knew there was no way they'd give out their number to any guy.

On the flip side, we've also been out with groups of girls who were dressed to kill in cleavage-revealing tops and micro minis that had full intentions of hooking-up that night, or at the very least giving out their phone numbers. It's so unfortunate that as guys we have no way to tell (even though we think we do) which women are out to meet guys. We think that the women who are dressed the skimpiest are the ones looking to meet guys. But as we've illustrated, this is not always the case.

Usually when you go out, fewer girls are looking to meet someone than you think. As we've discussed, there are a multitude of reasons why a girl would *not* want to be picked-up or even talked to: she may have a boyfriend, may have just gotten out of a relationship, may be there to meet up with a specific guy, might not be feeling well, might have just started dating someone. There's only one reason why she would want to meet you, and that's if she's single. Unfortunately, there are fewer single women out at night than you think.

Why are women out there, then, dressed so provocatively if they have a boyfriend and have no intentions of being picked-up? Because women *love* attention! Even women who are completely satisfied with their boyfriends, and who are not at all looking to meet a guy, love going out and getting attention. They love getting dressed up, and love the fact that every guy is looking at them, trying to talk to them, buying them drinks, trying to dance with them, asking for their phone number, and trying to hook-up with them.

It's unfortunate to us men that there's no way to tell which women are out to be picked-up, and which ones aren't. Once again, this is why we prefer to meet women either through friends of friends or at social events, because within minutes of meeting a girl we know her status. When girls meet you in an inviting environment, they will be honest and up-front with you about their situation. Or you can at least find it out through one of your mutual friends.

Let's now take a look at some common questions we're asked by guys:

Q: "Is your game so good that you can walk up to random girls on the street and pick them up?"

A: "Hell, no. Our game is simply good enough that we know better than to walk up to random girls on the street and try to pick them up. We know what low odds of success we have doing that, and thus we stay away from it."

Q: "So that girl in a bar who you said is not out to be picked-up, and not out to meet a guy, there's got to be something you can do—some secret, some magic— something you can do to pick her up?"

A: "Were you not listening to everything we just said? We just gave a bunch of reasons why that girl, even though she is so scantily clad, is *not* getting picked up tonight. For example, maybe she has a boyfriend whom she is loyal to and is in love with! How would you like it if you had a girlfriend or wife and some other guy had a magical formula to make her sleep with him?"

If you prefer to meet women in bothersome environments, then the most valuable advice we can offer you is to know when to move on. If you approach a girl and she is cold to you, and she's not giving you her attention (we'll talk more in the next chapter about approaching women), then move on. Don't make the mistake of thinking that you can make her talk to you. If she's cold to you, the best thing you can do is simply to assume that she has a boyfriend, and move on.

The problem is that we as guys are *always* looking to pick up a girl. So we assume that when women are out at night, they too are out to be picked up. But it's just not the case. No matter where you decide to meet women, however, the first step is having a good approach.

Chapter 4 – Approaching Women

So you're out and surrounded by women. But the first step in actually meeting a woman is walking over to her and starting a conversation. So what's the best approach? There is actually a distinct pattern to successful introductory conversation between a male and female, and here is how it should go:

Male: Open-ended Question #1
Female: Response #1
Male: Follow-up remark; follow-up question
Female: Response #2
Male: Follow-up remark; follow-up question
Female: Response #3
...
Male, extending right arm for handshake: "Oh, by the way, my name's <name>."
Female, completing handshake: "Hi, I'm <name>."
Male: Resume pattern with next question
...

This is the natural pattern of conversation that will keep your conversation flowing and her interested. So now the obvious question: What should Question #1 be? Well, forget all of those cheesy pickup lines. The best thing you can do is to look for a context clue. A context clue is something in the surrounding environment that you can easily ask her a question about. For example, if you see a girl wearing a University of Texas shirt, then your opening line can be:

"Hey, did/do you go to the University of Texas?"

The good thing about this question is that you can then use these follow-up questions if she did go to Texas:

"Cool, how did you like it?"
"Oh, what did you major in?"
"So what brought you to <city>?"

And if she didn't go to the University of Texas, you have these follow-up questions:

"Oh, where'd you get the shirt from?"
"Did you go to school around here then?"
"So are you from Texas?"

Or suppose you're in a bookstore, and a woman is reading a book entitled "The Beginner's Guide to Cooking." In this case, you can use the opening line:

"Oh, are you learning how to cook too?"

You can then proceed into a discussion on what types of food each of you like, what you already know how to cook, or even what your favorite dinner wines are.

Or suppose you're on the subway. You can always ask for directions:

"Excuse me, can you tell me how to get to Penn Station?"

The good thing about this line is that if the girl really seems to know, you can follow-up with:

"Thank you very much; have you lived here a while?"

Or if she doesn't seem to know, you can follow-up with:

"No, don't worry about it. Did you just move here?"

At parties, a great opening question is:

"So how do you know <host's name>?"

At bars, it's sometimes tough to find a context clue. In these cases, a simple question such as, "Are you originally from <this city>?" or "Do you live around here?" followed by, "What part of town do you live in?" can spark great conversation.

The key to choosing an opening question is that you want to make sure that it will spark insightful conversation. You'll notice we said that the opening question should be open-ended. An example of a bad question is:

"Rough weather we've been having, huh?"

This really only leaves her with one of two responses:

"Yeah, sure is"   or
"Nah, not so bad"

The other problem with that question is it doesn't show any interest in her as a person. The key to good conversation is asking good enough questions that they prompt long responses (not just "yes" or "no"), provoke good conversation, and allow her to open up to you. Learn to use the responses the woman gives to ask good follow-up questions. Of course, *don't* rapid-fire the questions. Let her talk, and give a follow-up response before asking the next question.

Sometimes it's difficult to find a context clue and come up with an opening question. That's why we have come up with a complete list of questions to memorize in case you can't think of anything to say. We've both memorized this list and had great success with it. We often find that by simply thinking of a few of these questions before approaching a girl, we can find a way to tie one of them into a context clue, as we have in the examples we just gave. We have reprinted this list in the Appendix for your use.

Here is an example of an opening sequence that one of us recently used in a coffee shop. We spotted a beautiful blonde wearing a UCLA sweatshirt, so we mentally pieced together this opening. All of the questions come from the list in the Appendix that we've memorized:

"Hey, did you go to UCLA?"

[If she didn't go to UCLA]
"Oh, where'd you go to school?"
"Why'd you move to LA?"
"Where are you originally from?"

[If she did go to UCLA]
"Cool! How'd you like it?"
"What did you study?"
"Are you originally from LA?"

Keep in mind that the point is *not* to rapid-fire questions. Ask the first question, let her answer, and give a follow-up remark. Then ask the next question. You should use these questions not only to start a conversation, but also to learn more about the activities she enjoys, so you can plan future dates. The conversation went well, although it turned out that she has a boyfriend.

Make sure you remember to go back and introduce yourself within the first few minutes of the conversation. You should extend your right hand for an introductory handshake as you do this, and confidently look her in the eyes (more on the importance of eye contact later in the chapter). Most women, when you do this, will complete the handshake and introduce themselves by name.

A Sample Conversation

We wanted to include a sample introductory conversation in this book, so we asked our student Jeremy to do us a favor. We asked him to go into a bar, walk up to a girl, and record the opening conversation. He agreed, and are we glad we asked. This was his first attempt of the evening, and he nailed it! He's actually playing tennis with her right now as we write this. And if they grab dinner afterward, this time we will *not* be taping the conversation. We have added our analysis, in brackets, to the conversation.

> Jeremy makes eye contact, and says with a smile: "Hey, how's it going?"
> Marissa: "Alright."
> Jeremy: "Are you from around here?"
> Marissa: "No, actually I grew up in New York."
> Jeremy: "Oh, so what brought you down here?"
> Marissa: "Well, I went to school at Duke, and was recruited to work here." [Gold mine! So many follow-up possibilities already. New York, Duke, where she works.]
> Jeremy: "Wow. Really!"
> Marissa: "Yeah, I'm working my way back up the Eastern seaboard, if you will."

Jeremy: "So how long have you lived in DC then?"

Marissa: "A little over two years now."

Jeremy: "OK, so you've been here for a little while now."

Marissa: "Yeah, I'm getting used to it."

Jeremy: "What do you think of it?"

Marissa: "It's nice, but it's no New York City. You do have the Metro, but it's definitely not the New York subway system! You sometimes have to do a lot of transferring lines just to go a short distance."

Jeremy: "Yeah, I know exactly what you mean. Just the other day I had to go somewhere in Maryland, and it's only 3 miles away, but taking the Metro would have required switching lines, and driving on the beltway isn't much fun either!" [Good follow-up remark—shows he can relate to her, but doesn't dominate the conversation.]

Marissa: "Yeah, I try to avoid the beltway at all costs. I'm just not good driving in traffic!"

Jeremy: "So what part of town do you live in?"

Marissa: "I live out in Fairfax. So I sometimes get too lazy to come into the city to go out! Where do you live?" [Good—she asked a question about him. We know she's not trying to get rid of him.]

Jeremy: "I live in Arlington, which is nice because I can walk to a few bars, or take the Metro over to Clarendon during the week. So what part of town do you normally go out in?"

Marissa: "Ah, usually either Clarendon or DC. I like Clarendon because it's a lot closer and I don't have to deal with all of the DC traffic."

Jeremy: "Yeah, I know what you mean—living off of the Metro line, I guess you have to drive anytime you want to go out."

Marissa: "Yeah, but it's really not that far. It's just getting up the motivation to get into the car and make the trek. Especially this time of year, the cold weather is a real deterrent. Then again, back home I have to drive to go out anywhere. So I'm used to it." [Mental notes: Doesn't like driving on the beltway; doesn't like trekking out by car—pick her up for all dates.]

Marissa: "I also really like that pool place in Clarendon."

Jeremy: "Star Billiards?"

Marissa: "Yeah!"

Jeremy: "You shoot pool?"

Marissa: "Well, I'm not that good, but I love playing pool!"

Jeremy: "Yeah, I really like that place." [Mental note for future date: likes pool; likes Star Billiards]

Jeremy, extending right arm for handshake: "Oh, I'm Jeremy, by the way."

Marissa, completing handshake and smiling: "Hi, Jeremy. My name's Marissa."

Jeremy: "Yeah, so do you actually live in the city—in New York City?" [found out where she likes to go out & hit a dead-end; switch topics to NYC]

Marissa: "No, about half an hour away; 45 minutes away from it."

Jeremy: "Oh, what part of New York City?"

Marissa: "You mean what part of New York?"

Jeremy: "Oh yeah, sorry—you just told me you live outside the city." [covering-up the fact that he forgot to listen to her previous answer]

Marissa: "In Valhalla. In the White Plains area."

Jeremy: "Oh, is that in Westchester?"

Marissa: "Yeah."

Jeremy: "Oh, OK. I don't actually know much about Westchester, but I have some family up there."

Marissa: "Oh, really? Where at?"

Jeremy: "Um... I don't know... All I know is Westchester County."

Marissa: "Yeah, Westchester County is pretty big. I think it's made a name for itself." [Realizes he's hit a dead-end—doesn't know enough about Westchester Co. to continue with this topic; switches topics]

Jeremy: "Yeah, it definitely has. So, where'd you say you went to school again?"

Marissa: "Duke."

Jeremy: "Yeah, that's what I thought." [Tries to cover up the fact that he's completely forgotten where she went to school.]

Jeremy: "So, if you're from New York, what brought you down South?" [Has multiple angles—could have asked questions about the school itself; saving that angle for later.]

Marissa: "Well, one of my friends went there. And her father went there. So she convinced me to come visit. I was really looking for schools up in the Boston area..."

Jeremy: "What other schools did you look at?"

Marissa: "I looked at BC, and some of the Ivy schools, but decided I didn't necessarily want to go to an Ivy League school."

Jeremy: "Yeah, I know what you mean." [Shows her that he's listening, but let's her finish her thought.]

Marissa: "I just didn't want the stigma, and now, looking back on it, I think it would have been a good decision. But coming out of high school, and working my tail off in high school, I didn't necessarily want to go that route. So I was really looking for a really good school, without all of the stigma of an Ivy."

Jeremy: "Yeah, I completely understand." [Yep, I'm listening. Keep talking.]

Marissa: "So I applied there, I applied to Emory too because I've always wanted to go there as a kid. But then went and visited and didn't like it at all!"

Jeremy: "Yeah, I know what you mean."

Marissa: "There's just something about it, and I figure—if you get a bad feeling..." [This is great—her responses are getting longer—she's interested in talking.]

Jeremy: "Yeah, if you get a bad feeling from visiting, then you probably don't want to go there. So how did you like Duke?"

Marissa: "I liked it. I liked it a lot when I went to visit. And I like the class sizes, because it seemed like I would get a lot of attention. And it worked out well for me. Because I wound up majoring in psychology, and it's one of the top psychology programs in the nation."

Jeremy: "How was the psych. program there? Did you like it?"

Marissa: "I did. I wound up doing an honors program there. Not to sound like a little nerd, or anything."

Jeremy: "Of course not! That's really cool, actually!" [Realizing that she's smart too! Wow! Hot and smart!]

Marissa: "You don't automatically get in just based on GPA. You have to apply and be accepted in. "

Jeremy: "My brother was in one of those programs, too. "

Marissa: "It's really cool. I mean, I would have dinner at the head of the department's house, so you really get 'in' with the department by doing it. It was a good experience. Looking back on it now, because of knowing what I know now, and working with people who went to a bunch of different schools, I think I would want to go to a big state school with lots of sports, just for a different experience."

Jeremy: "Is Duke a private school?"

Marissa: "Yeah."

Jeremy: "Duke's got good sports though."

Marissa: "Yeah, but it doesn't have the football excitement of say, an Ohio State or a Michigan."

Jeremy: "How many people go to Duke?" [We'll come back to the sports thing in just a second.]

Marissa: "Around 6,000 undergrads."

Jeremy: "Oh, OK. So it's a lot smaller than I thought."

Marissa: "Yeah, everyone thinks it's really big. Just because it's an ACC school. Wake's actually not that big either."

Jeremy: "So did you go to basketball games while you were there?"

Marissa: "Yeah, I got to see Shane Battier."

Jeremy: "Oh, that's cool! Do you follow sports in general?"

Marissa: "Yeah, I love sports. I love playing, I love watching." [Oh, man. Dream girl. Mental note for future date: invite her to Skins or Caps game?]

Jeremy: "Really, what's your favorite sport? What sports do you like to watch? What do you like to play?"

Marissa: "Uh..." [Jeremy realizes he's just gotten over-excited and rapid-fired too many questions]

Jeremy: "I'm sorry. What's your main sport that you play?"

Marissa: "Basketball. I would say basketball. I played sports all through high school and wasn't quite talented enough to play basketball in Division I ACC, of all places. I played a couple sports."

Jeremy: "Do you ever play tennis?"

Marissa: "Yeah, I played in high school, actually." [Hell, yes. The #1 sport to play with a girl.]

Jeremy: "Oh, that's cool! I'm always looking for someone to play tennis with. I'm no expert, but I love to play."

Marissa: "Yeah, I haven't played consistently in years, so I'm sure we're at the same level."

Jeremy: "You'd probably beat me, but it'd still be a lot of fun."

Marissa: "I think it'd be a lot of fun! We should play sometime!" [Hell, yes. She made the offer. She obviously feels quite comfortable around Jeremy—already.]

Jeremy: "Oh, absolutely."

Marissa: "It'll be fun."

Jeremy: "Well, it'll be fun until you start beating me."

Marissa: "Are you the competitive type?"

Jeremy: "I'm not overly competitive. I just play for fun—because I enjoy it."

Marissa: "OK, then it'll be a lot of fun!" [Got what he wanted out of this part of the conversation; hit a dead-end, so switch topics.]

Jeremy: "So did you move to DC straight from Duke?"

Marissa: "Well, I went to Europe over the summer, but then moved to DC and started working."

Jeremy: "Really? Where'd you go in Europe?"

Marissa: "All over France, England, and Italy. That's where I got this necklace."

Jeremy: "Yeah, I've been admiring that—that is *really* pretty."

Marissa, smiling brightly: "Thank you!" [Yes. Great compliment.]

Jeremy: "Where did you get the necklace?"

Marissa: "At this cute little place in Paris. I love it because every time I look at it, it reminds me of Paris!"

Jeremy: "How long were you in Europe for?"

Marissa: "Only four weeks; then I had to come back and start work."

Jeremy: "Ah. Where do you work?" [Doesn't know much about Europe; good transition to new topic.]

Marissa: "At Mortgage Installment Financial."

Jeremy: "Yeah, out in Falls Church, right?"

Marissa: "Yep, the big building that you pass on I-66."

Jeremy: "What do you do there?"

Marissa: "I'm an internal consultant, basically selling strategy internally."

Jeremy: "Huh, did you think about working for any of the big consulting companies?"

Marissa: "I applied to a couple of them, but got cut after second-round interviews." [Jeremy realizes he's starting to hit a dead-end here talking about her career, and realizes that he probably wouldn't understand what she does at work anyway.]

Jeremy: "So what was it like growing up in New York City? Well, technically not in New York City. But, right outside?"

Marissa: "You know, I think I never got old enough to fully enjoy it. I was never 21 in New York City, since I went away to college. But I got to enjoy it a little bit cause when I lived with my parents they'd let me take the train into the city by myself."

Jeremy: "Yeah, I know what you mean because, growing up in DC, I was never old enough to go out here. So I never really learned where people go out until I moved back here after college."

Marissa: "Exactly. Until you reach a certain age, I think every childhood experience is the same. I mean—you go to hang out at someone's house, and then you're old enough to go to the movies, or go hang out at the mall, or do typical teenage activities. But no matter where you grow up, you really don't go out until you hit college age."

Jeremy: "Yeah, definitely."

Marissa: "It was cool, though. My friends and I got really involved in music. So we would go to concerts a lot." [Conversation's going well. She's naturally transitioning to new topics.]

Jeremy: "Oh, wow. You must've gone to a lot of concerts. I mean, everyone comes through New York."

Marissa: "Yeah, so we got lucky in that respect. So I guess I got to enjoy it a little bit. I kind of got spoiled by it. Moving to North Carolina, we really didn't get many concerts. One of the best concerts I've ever been to is Springsteen—oh, it was so much fun!" [Mental note for future date: Springsteen's coming to town. Find out later what other bands she likes]

Jeremy: "Well, hey. My friends look pretty bored over there, so I should get back to them. But it was nice meeting you, Marissa."

Jeremy extends his hand for a closing handshake.

Marissa, extending her hand to complete the handshake: "It was really nice meeting you, too."

Jeremy: "And we should definitely play tennis sometime. Can I get your e-mail address?"

Marissa: "Of course!" She writes it down on a napkin and hands it to him.

Jeremy: "Great! Well, talk to you later. Have a nice evening!"

Marissa: "You too—go liven up your friends!"

Jeremy: "Absolutely!"

Jeremy then went into the bathroom, let out a *huge* grin that he'd been concealing for fifteen minutes, and jotted down some notes on the cocktail napkin with Marissa's e-mail address: "tennis, loves sports—Skins or Caps game?, Springsteen concert?, Star Billiards? Off Metro line—I drive for all dates. Went to Duke; from NYC; Pysch major"

Jeremy next used e-mail to start a casual dialogue with her, and to set up their tennis match (more on this in the next chapter). Through e-mail, he later found out more about things she enjoys. For example, he found out that she loves going to hockey, football and baseball games, but thinks professional basketball is boring (good thing he didn't get Wizards tickets).

Notice how Jeremy used the questions he asked to steer the conversation and find out about her interests. This will help him immensely in planning dates. If tennis goes well, he plans to shoot pool with her sometime next week, and invite her to Springsteen in three weeks. See what you can learn from a great opening conversation!

To be fair, we'll also include another attempt Jeremy made. This girl, obviously, did *not* want to talk to Jeremy. Luckily, Jeremy knows there's nothing you can do about this in a bar environment, and he *never* takes it personally:

Jeremy makes eye contact, and says with a smile: "Hey, how's it going?"

Woman: "OK."

Jeremy: "Are you from around here?"

Woman: "All my life."

Jeremy: "Yeah, I grew up here too. What part of town did you grow up in?"

Woman: "Reston."

Jeremy: "Ah, I grew up in Maryland. Do you still live out in Reston?"

Woman: "Yep."

Jeremy: "Did you go to school around here?"

Woman: "Yep."

Jeremy, trying to stay positive: "Cool. Where at?"

Woman: "American."

Jeremy: "I've heard it's a fun school. Did you like it?"

Woman, turning away from him: "It was alright."

Jeremy: "Well, I'm gonna get back to my friends—they look pretty bored. But it was really nice meeting you."

Jeremy later expressed to us that he thought having his wisdom teeth pulled was slightly less painful than conversation with this woman. Sometimes you just have to accept that, for whatever reason, a particular girl doesn't want to talk to you right now. Don't take it personally. Just move on.

First Impressions: Asking questions and exuding confidence

Conventional wisdom says that first impressions are very important. And, in many ways, CCR is about taking the art of making a good first impression to a higher level.

Don't try to impress women with the clothes you wear, the car you drive, your bulging biceps, or your Ivy League vocabulary. This doesn't do it. What impresses a girl when you first meet her is the interest that you show in her, not sexually, but in her as a person. Make it your goal when you first meet a woman to find out: what makes her happy; what she enjoys doing; how she *feels* about her job; what she's studying. Showing genuine interest in a woman will get you further with her than any tale about scoring the winning touchdown ever will.

As we're about to discuss, confidence is crucial, and it's something that you really can't fake. When you are confident, you don't need to talk about yourself. You don't need to show your muscles. You don't need to use big words to sound like you're smart. You're secure and comfortable with who you are, and that is attractive to women. We always used to try to be the center of attention at parties by being loud and sarcastic. We never became friends with women and, frankly, we never got laid. We acted immaturely because we were insecure and lacked confidence. Once we started approaching things as suggested, people responded more favorably to us, our confidence grew, and a positive cycle began—confidence breeding more confidence.

Here's a conversation we overheard two female friends having about a random guy at a party. Sadly, it's great insight about the first impressions that many of us leave:

Sarah: "What do you think of Brad?"
Jane: "He's funny, but I don't know if I could be around him all the time. You can only take his sense of humor in small doses. He'd get annoying fast. He's just such a guy... showing off, trying to be cute.... He was checking out my sparkly pants and said he couldn't find Mars among the constellations, but he's still looking for Uranus."
Sarah: "What a vulgar idiot."
Jane: "It's vintage Brad. I know he was trying to be funny, but it's just annoying. I wish

guys wouldn't try so damn hard to impress women."
Sarah: "Good luck trying to find one."

Guys who deliberately act funny or cool obviously don't impress Sarah and Jane. In fact, guys behave this way so frequently that Sarah and Jane see this as the "norm." Finding a guy that approaches the world and women differently would be a miracle for them. We can't tell you how great a feeling it was when women we met started responding positively to us because we didn't try showing off. We simply asked them questions about themselves and took a genuine interest in learning more about them.

Reticence

This element of a good first impression may be difficult for many men: the concept of reticence, or keeping your opinions to yourself (at first). If she loved a certain movie that you hated, don't bother telling her. Things you see as minor differences can appear as a sign of incompatibility to a woman. And most women don't want to take a chance on a guy they're not compatible with. It is best to refrain from expressing your opinions when you have first met a girl, as such trivial things as your favorite movies can scare her off. Simply don't offer up your opinion on anything.

A good example of this is women who are dog lovers. These women would never give a guy who dislikes dogs a chance. Why risk missing out on a great opportunity with a beautiful woman because you expressed an opinion too early? This missed opportunity we witnessed at a party says it all:

Anne: "Oh, look. Sheila's dog is wearing the cutest little doggie jacket."
Shawn: "I hate that. Why would you waste your money on a jacket for a dumb dog?

Doesn't she have anything better to spend her money on? And it just looks so ridiculous."

Shawn walked away, and Anne's friend Carol walked up.

Anne: "Do you know Shawn? Are you good friends with him?"

Carol: "I don't know him that well."

Anne: "He seems cruel or jaded or something. He said he hates dogs in doggie jackets. How can you hate that? It's so cute. I'm thinking about getting one for Barkley for Christmas, a red and green jacket with reindeer on it."

Carol: "Barkley will look so cute in that. I can't believe Shawn said that."

Anne: "I know. I was kind of into him until that."

One final point about reticence. Are we saying to walk around being a shallow person with no opinion on anything? No, not at all. We're simply advising you to, unlike most men, withhold on your opinions the first couple of times that you're around a woman, until you get to know her a little better.

Eye Contact

How do you convey to a woman that you are truly listening to her, understanding her, and internalizing what she is saying? Two words: eye contact.

When you're talking to a girl, presumably because you're asking her a question, talk directly to her. Many guys we know talk loudly enough for the entire room to hear (probably because they're talking about themselves). Women prefer it when you look directly into their eyes and talk quietly, as if they're the only person in the room. No one else needs to hear what the two of you are talking about. Talk to a person, not to a room.

You will occasionally need to break eye contact or you will freak her out. But for the most part, the idea is to focus on her and not get distracted. Don't look at the television. Don't look around the bar. Don't check out the rest of her body. Don't look at her breasts. Definitely don't look at other women. Look at her. The deeper into her eyes that she thinks you are looking, the more she'll want you. Maintain long, thoughtful gazes.

A good tip for sustained, interested eye contact is to pick one eye and focus on it. If you have ever made eye contact with someone who is alternating back and forth between your eyes, you know that it is quite unnerving. But a deep look into one of her eyes, not at the bridge of her nose or anywhere else on her face, will be interpreted by a woman as the beginnings of a connection. Our friend Patricia had this to say about the effects of eye contact:

> "I find deep eye contact *so* sexy. I love it when a guy stares into my eyes. It reassures me that he's really listening and he cares about what I'm saying."

A final note about eye contact: make it your goal to memorize the eye color of every girl you meet. Think about it. You can recall the hair length, hair color, facial structure, body structure, breast size, height, weight, and inseam of every girl you've ever met. You probably don't remember a single girl's eye color.

What's the point of memorizing a woman's eye color? Two reasons. First, it forces you to make intense eye contact. While you're working on storing the eye color in your memory, you'll be staring so deeply into her eyes that she'll think you lost something in there. The other point is to recall her eye color at a later time when you're not looking at her eyes (on the phone, over e-mail, or in a room with the lights out). Women are highly impressed when you tell them over the phone:

> "Of course I remember meeting you at Shawn's party. You have those incredible blue eyes."

Attitude

Attitude is crucial. We never used to think much of those motivational speakers or those omnipresent motivational quotes, but we now recognize their validity. Maintaining a positive, upbeat and enthusiastic attitude is crucial to being a Man of CCR. All of the compliments, compassion and reassurance in the world will not do you a bit of good without the right attitude. In fact, the only time you shouldn't have an upbeat attitude is when you're listening to a woman's sad or problematic story. In which case, as previously mentioned, you should match the storyteller's emotions.

Enthusiasm

If you are to be a successful Man of CCR, there's only one attitude that will work, and that's a positive, upbeat manner. Remember that the keys to making a girl like you are showing that you like who she is as a person, and making her like herself; negativity is not going to achieve this objective.

Don't complain about anything when you've first met a woman. Any small comment can be misconstrued as a giant complaint. We were in an elevator the other day with a guy who said, "Man, these buttons always stick." The woman with him responded, "George, you just complain about everything." Before CCR, we never would have considered George's comment a complaint. Now that we are aware of how sensitive women are to negativity, we realize the importance of keeping our comments in check. The bottom line: if the elevator button is sticky, there's absolutely no point in mentioning it.

If your life is stressful and you have a lot to complain about, voice all of your complaints to your male friends. Tell them everything, get it out of your system, and don't say a negative word around women.

Crass, offensive and sexually rude comments or jokes also serve no purpose. Women are easily offended. Don't risk upsetting anyone. Knowing that every woman will love you should be far more rewarding than the thrill you get from making an occasional crass comment. Save the sexual and bathroom humor for the guys.

This story illustrates the point that women notice and like positive guys:

> Lucy: "I ran into Mike the other day."
> Dave: "Mike's awesome. How's he doing?"
> Teresa: "You know something, Dave? You never have anything bad to say about anyone. You get along with everyone."
> Jennie: "Yeah, I've noticed that too. You seem to genuinely like everyone."
> Lucy: "I've never met anyone who gets along so well with everyone."
> Joan: "Me either."
> Jennie: "Yeah, me either."
> Joan: "It's really cool."
> Jennie: "We should all be like that. People are so petty in this world and dislike others for the smallest reasons."
> Joan: "I know. I guess that's part of the reason why everybody likes you so much, Dave."

As you can see, girls love a guy who never bad-mouths anyone and always maintains a positive attitude.

As difficult as it may be at times, never complain about your job. You spend half of your waking hours at work so do your best to find a job that you love. If you do, your overall attitude will be far superior to that of someone who dislikes his job.

Like it or not, your career is a major reflection of who you are as a person. Women are highly impressed by a man who responds enthusiastically to questions about his job. It shows that he really has his life together, and it adds to a man's overall confidence. Our friend April had this to say about guys who like their job:

> "It really impresses me when a guy likes his job. I don't know what it is, but he just seems to exude a certain confidence. He obviously went out and sought out a job that he knew he would like, and he met his goal. This translates into a certain type of masculine security in a man."

Confidence

This brings us to the most important part of attitude: confidence. Why did we wait so long to talk about confidence if it's the most important part of being a Man of CCR? Because by implementing CCR you will naturally gain confidence. It is the difference between simply being a counselor to women, and being someone they want. You can offer compliments, compassion and reassurance all day long, but if you aren't secure with yourself few women will ever want you.

Why do women love confidence? The reason for it is simple: it makes them feel secure. Women certainly picked an interesting characteristic to be so fond of. Confidence is the one thing you can't fake. It's true that success breeds confidence, which in turn breeds more success, and this is something that makes women feel secure in choosing to be around you or with you.

How do you build confidence? Well, neither of us was particularly confident before CCR. This was because neither of us had had all that much success with women. But when we started practicing CCR, the most amazing thing started happening: women truly wanted to be around us all the time. They genuinely loved being around us!

If you don't have confidence, don't try to fake it. Accept that you have only had limited success with women, and realize that your confidence will grow over time. Keep in mind that there's a difference between confidence and cockiness. Every other piece of literature we've read tells guys that to "get" the girl you've got to have an air of cockiness about you. They claim that once you enter the *friend zone* with a female your chances of sleeping with her are doomed. This is an extremely short-sighted view.

Remember, other than Men of CCR, girls are attracted to 3 types of guys:

1. Good-looking guys
2. Rich guys
3. Famous guys (or even local celebrities)

One of the biggest misconceptions that guys have is that girls like jerks. Guys think that by trying to be cocky and arrogant girls will like them. As we discussed in the chapter "What is CCR?", the truth is that girls like guys because they fit into one or more of the categories above. Once they like a guy because he is hot, rich or famous, the guy can get away with being a bit of a jerk and the girl will still like him. She likes him less, but not enough to deter her from being with a hot, rich, or famous guy. The bottom line is that it's not the jerk part of the guy they go for; it's the category he's in.

Once you learn CCR it will change your attitude forever. You should use it in every social setting. As this story relates, you never know who's watching:

> Mike flew from Chicago to his hometown in Florida to attend a wedding. He figured it

would be cool, and it would give him a chance to see people he hadn't seen since graduating from high school 8 years ago. Long before he was a Man of CCR.

He realized he had a choice to make while he was away: regress into his former self, making crass comments like he used to in high school, or continue his new life as a Man of CCR. He wouldn't see these people again for years, if ever again. Mike decided, however, that CCR behavior was the way to go.

The wedding was a blast. He saw a lot of old friends, and many of the girls were impressed that he was so complimentary of them. Mike came back to Chicago in a great mood, knowing that he had impressed everyone.

Back in Chicago Monday morning, Mike got an e-mail from Anne, a girl he vaguely knew in high school. She was absolutely beautiful in high school, a cheerleader who was also on the gymnastics team. Back then, he wouldn't have had a shot in hell with her. The e-mail read:

Hey, Mike. I don't know if you remember me from high school or not, but I just got an e-mail from Kellie. She & I have kept in touch over the years. Anyway, Kellie said she saw you at Mike & Susan's wedding & that she really enjoyed talking to you. She told me that you live in Chicago now, as do I! Hopefully we can get together some time & catch up. Hope things are going well :)

Anne

And this is why you should be a Man of CCR in *every* social setting.

A final point about attitude: be careful of the "cute" little comments that you make. Women might not find them so cute. Our friend Amanda had this to say about her tongue ring:

> "Every guy who sees my tongue ring always says, 'Is that to enhance oral sex?' That's so immature. I like it and I think it's cool. That's it. And you know what? I haven't gone down on any guy since I've had it. And you know why? Because every guy thinks that's why I got it. When I finally meet a guy who doesn't comment that he thinks I got the tongue ring for oral sex, he'll be the first."

Our friend Laura had this to say about being from Beverly Hills:

> "When guys hear that I'm from Beverly Hills, they always say, 'Oh, you must be rich. Let's get married.' It's just so insulting to even think that a guy even cares about how much money my family or I have, especially when we've just met. And to make a comment like, 'Let's get married.' That just tells me that the guy isn't interested in things that matter, like love. He just wants me for my money. It's such a turn-off."

Just keep in mind that what you consider to be a cute comment or an innocent joke might not be interpreted that way by a woman. Use the *Golden Rule of CCR*: If you don't have anything CCR to say, don't say anything at all!

Chapter 5 – Getting Contact Info and Making Future Contact

How many times have you or one of your friends talked to a girl, had great conversation with her, yet left without getting her contact info? We've done it dozens of times ourselves, and yet there's no reason for it. You're so happy that you met a really cool girl and had great conversation; yet you spend the rest of the evening (and often the next day) kicking yourself for not having the nerve to ask for her contact info.

Why does this happen? Because asking a girl for her contact info is a gut-wrenching process. It requires you to put your neck on the line, to put yourself out there and risk getting shot down. What if there were a way to make it less gut-wrenching, a way to make it less of a risk? A way to make it so comfortable and casual that you do not even think twice about doing it?

Let's look back at how Jeremy, in the previous chapter, asked Marissa for her contact info:

Jeremy: "Well, hey. My friends look pretty bored over there, so I should get back to them. But it was nice meeting you, Marissa."

Jeremy extends his hand for a closing handshake.

Marissa, extending her hand to complete the handshake: "It was really nice meeting you, too."

Jeremy: "And we should definitely play tennis sometime. Can I get your e-mail address?"

Marissa: "Of course!" She writes it down on a napkin and hands it to him.

Jeremy: "Great! Well, talk to you later. Have a nice evening!"

Marissa: "You too—go liven up your friends!"

Jeremy: "Absolutely!"

Why was this so natural and easy for Jeremy? Because he had a reason to ask for her contact info. He had already established ten minutes ago that they would play tennis sometime; now it was merely up to him to get her contact info so that they could arrange a match. When you're talking to a girl, make the point of using the conversation to find out as many things as possible that can translate into tangible date ideas. Use the questions in the Appendix to naturally steer the conversation toward her interests.

The introductory conversation doesn't have to be long. You can keep it to ten, fifteen, twenty minutes, and still have an effective conversation. In Jeremy's fifteen-minute conversation, he found out that Marissa likes to play tennis; likes sports; likes to shoot pool, especially at Star Billiards; and that she likes Springsteen.

During the conversation, pick out one thing in particular and try to establish it as something that the two of you should do together. Let's look again at how Jeremy did this:

Jeremy: "Do you ever play tennis?"

Marissa: "Yeah, I played in high school, actually."
Jeremy: "Oh, that's cool! I'm always looking for someone to play tennis with. I'm no expert, but I love to play."
Marissa: "Yeah, I haven't played consistently in years, so I'm sure we're at the same level."
Jeremy: "You'd probably beat me, but it'd still be a lot of fun."
Marissa: "I think it'd be a lot of fun! We should play sometime!"

Let's analyze what Jeremy did to establish that they should play tennis together. It was a four-step process.

Step #1: Find a common interest.
Step #2: Show that you're excited about this common interest.
Step #3: State that you're always looking for someone to share that activity with.
Step #4: Very casually, offer that it would be fun if the two of you got together sometime to participate in that activity.

Here are some other examples, using other activities:

"Oh, cool—I love shooting pool. I'm always looking for someone to go shoot pool with ... [let her respond] ... We should go shoot pool some time!"

"Oh, wow—I've always wanted to go see a play there ... [let her respond] ... We should go see a play there some time—it'd be a lot of fun!"

"Yeah, I've always wanted to go to one of the nearby vineyards ... [let her respond] ... We should go wine-tasting one afternoon when the weather's nice out!"

Don't feel the need to gather her contact info at that exact moment. Keep the conversation flowing, to show her that you're interested in her as a person.

At the end of the conversation, when you're ready to ask for her contact info, don't make a big deal out of it. Just ask.

> "We should definitely [play tennis / shoot pool / see a play / go wine-tasting] some time! Can I get your [e-mail address / phone number]?"

It's really that simple.

Relinquishing Short-Term Sexual Desire

Notice how casual the request for contact information was. We can't emphasize enough the need for casualness in the early stages of interaction. You do not want to intimidate and scare the girl in any way. Women want to know that you are interested in them as a person, *not* as a sex object. Remember, you want to spend time with her because she is cool, fun, and/or smart, *not* because you want to sleep with her.

Most guys are very aggressive when they pursue women. The night that Jeremy met Marissa, he didn't hit on her, didn't try to take her home, didn't try to sleep with her, and didn't try to set up a date. He merely made great conversation, found out about Marissa's interests, established a mutual interest, and asked for her contact info so that they can get together to play tennis.

This impresses women. An extremely good-looking friend of ours, Katie, had this to say about getting "hit on":

> "I actually find it sexy when a guy doesn't hit on me. Because I get hit on all the time, and I can tell by the way a guy looks at me that

all he wants to do is sleep with me. I would love to just meet a guy who's interested in me for me and doesn't have a single objective on his little mind. That's the kind of guy I want to meet."

The hotter the woman, the more impressed she'll be if you show interest in her as a person. Hot women are used to guys in aggressive pursuit. They're used to every guy wanting them. When you play it cool, it's a new experience for her, and she'll find it intriguing. She'll wonder why you're not hitting on her and find you a challenge. This, in turn, makes her want you.

Whenever we start teaching CCR to other guys, we always hear the same questions:

"Won't girls see through things like constant complimenting?"

"Won't girls think it's odd that I'm showing so much interest in her, and not talking about myself?"

What we tell them is the following:

"The key to CCR is sincerity. If you go around complimenting girls constantly, and you don't mean it, they will see right through it. But if you sincerely keep a positive, upbeat attitude while practicing CCR, they will be *amazed*. Go ahead, just give it a try. So few guys actually compliment women. If guys knew how a simple compliment could equate to success with women, they would all start. Try it and watch how women react to you."

Our pupils always come back to us with something along the lines of:

"OK, I was completely skeptical. But I figured I'd give it a try. I met this girl at a bar the other day. I kept a really positive attitude, complimented her, and had a great conversation. I found out some of her interests, and showed compassion when she was complaining

79

about her apartment. And you know what? At the end of the conversation, she told me how much fun she'd had chatting with me. She even *gave* me her e-mail address so we could get together for sushi."

Planning the Date

Remember all the questions you're supposed to ask a woman when you first meet her? And remember that you're supposed to *really* listen? By doing these things, you've not only made a positive connection in the woman's mind, you have also learned about which activities she enjoys the most, so you can spend more time with her.

With this said, let's focus on what you should do during dates. One of the main problems that guys have is that no one ever teaches us the proper way to date. There's no course in school, and our fathers usually don't teach us, not that they actually know anyway. What little we do know about dating we usually learn from watching TV, but that mostly shows guys inviting girls to dinner and a movie. We're now about to tell you what exactly women are looking for on a date. This knowledge will not only help you have more successful dates, but also make you much more confident on a date.

When planning a date, try to pick activities that meet these two criteria:

1. The activity should be fun and interesting to the woman.
2. The event should be casual so that you can both relax, have great conversation, and connect.

One important thing that never occurs to most guys is making the woman feel as relaxed and comfortable around you as possible. Most guys don't realize this, but women are often very intimidated and untrusting of men's intentions (and can you blame them?). This is why we always encourage the first few dates to be in public, relaxed environments, to help the woman relax around you and become more comfortable around you.

As you'll notice, a lot of what we talk about is focused on making the woman more relaxed around us, and more trusting of us. Ultimately, in order for two people to connect, they have to feel comfortable around each other and they have to trust one another. This is something important that most guys don't realize.

With this in mind, look at the date not as a date, but rather as two people hanging out, spending time together, and getting to know each other better. Dates are awkward and uncomfortable, and no one really likes them. Simply viewing a date differently can really change your approach to dating in general. When we started viewing dates in this manner, it completely changed our mindset.

How much money you spend on a girl during a date does not matter, either. The fact that money matters on dates is a huge myth, which causes a lot of guys to waste tons of money trying to impress the woman. Listen to the following conversation between our friends Melissa and Laura about the dates they had gone on the night before:

Melissa: "So how was your date?"

Laura: "Oh, it was nice. We went out to this fancy French restaurant. I had this great seafood dish, and we split a bottle of red wine, which was really good. Afterward, we went to see a movie. Overall, the date was all right. I mean, dinner was really good, the wine was nice, and the movie was fun. But, you know, I just didn't feel like we were really connecting."

Melissa: "Did you get any action?!"

Laura: "No, but afterward he leaned in to kiss me goodnight. I let him, because I felt obligated. But there was no way I was inviting him inside. I could just tell that we were two different people, and that we weren't connecting."

Melissa: "That's too bad. I'm so sorry. Do you think he'll call you again?"

Laura: "I'm sure he will. The bad ones always do. I'll just do what we usually do though."

Melissa: "Lie and tell him that your ex-boyfriend called this week and you're really confused and don't want to start anything up right now with anyone?"

Laura: "Yep. Why do guys suck so bad?"

Melissa: "Well, I think I've found one who doesn't suck."

Laura, shocked: "Really! How was *your* date?"

Melissa: "It was incredible!"

Laura, "Tell me, tell me!"

Melissa: "OK. He invited me to go for a walk in the park. It was *so* great. It was such a beautiful day out, and the sun was shining. We took a walk though the park, and the conversation just flowed so naturally. You could tell that we really understood each other.

I told him all about myself, and shared so much—and he was so interested in me. He kept asking me questions—not just to ask—but I could tell he was really interested. The conversation wasn't forced at all. We totally connected!"

Laura: "So what did you do in the park?"

Melissa: "Oh, they had this beautiful flower garden there, so we walked down through it. It was really pretty. As we were walking through the flower garden, he looked me right in the eyes and told me how beautiful I looked today—I'll never forget that. And there was a petting zoo so we walked through and fed some of the animals. It was so much fun—I felt like a kid again. Carl is just such a really fun-loving, laid-back guy. And the best thing about him is that I have fun with him without having to really do anything. I mean, that's the kind of guy I want—a guy who I can have fun with, and who makes me feel good about myself—no matter where I'm at."

Laura: "That's so amazing!"

Melissa: "But it got even better."

Laura: "Do tell."

Melissa: "As it got later in the afternoon, the sun was about to set. So Carl asked me if I'd like to split a bottle of wine with him underneath an oak tree and watch the sunset."

Laura: "How can you turn that down!"

Melissa: "I couldn't. So we went into the gift shop, and he bought a bottle of red wine. He even got them to open it for us, and got a couple of plastic cups. And we went out and sat underneath the oak tree and watched the sunset. It was *so* amazing!"

Laura: "Oooooooohhhhhh! I'm SO jealous! Why did *you* get to meet him?"

The most important thing is how well you connect with a girl, and how much fun the two of you have, *not* how much money you spend on her. Notice how Melissa was even impressed by Carl's resourcefulness in finding plastic cups to use. Laura's date spent $90 on dinner, and another $20 at the movies. That's $110 for a kiss goodnight, and no second date. Carl bought an $8 bottle of wine, and can have as many future dates as he wants with Melissa.

Inevitably when we present this in our courses, someone always says, "Oh, I know girls who won't go out with you unless you take them out to a $100 dinner." OK. There are exceptions. There are some women who care about money above all else, and who won't go out with you unless you lavish them with gifts and spend hundreds of dollars. However, we believe that this type of girl is the minority. And is this the type of girl you really want to date, and possibly worse, marry, anyway?

When you're planning the activity, ensure that it will allow the two of you to have great conversation and focus on the connection. As you've just seen, a walk in the park with great conversation goes over a million times better than a nice dinner at a French restaurant with average conversation.

Since great conversation and a connection are so important, you can also see the importance of holding your dates in a non-intimidating environment. We strongly feel that hanging out at a park on a beautiful afternoon or grabbing a cup of coffee is much less intimidating than a dinner date at a French restaurant. Because this environment is less intimidating, you will both be more relaxed, and thus more likely to connect through great conversation.

So many guys think that they're impressing a woman by taking her out to a nice dinner, when actually they'd have a much higher success rate by simply going out for dessert the first time out, and it would save them $100 to boot. Save the French restaurant for when the two of you are seriously dating, so you can actually enjoy the food in comfort.

So how do you choose what casual event to invite a girl to do on a first date? Invite her to do things that you know, from previous conversation, interest her. For example, we already stated that Jeremy played tennis with Marissa the first time they got together. Jeremy next plans to invite Marissa to Star Billiards, and then to see Springsteen in concert. These activities will show Marissa that Jeremy actually listened to what she said, which is huge to a woman.

We recently introduced our friend Cindy to one of our students, Rick, now a Man of CCR. She had this to say about him after they had gone out on a few dates:

> "I couldn't believe that Rick invited me to go for a bike ride, go to a museum, and watch a polo match. I mean, sure I had told him how much I enjoy all of those things. But most guys *still* invite you to dinner and a movie, and just ignore the things you tell them interest you. That's why Rick is so amazing—he actually listens to what I say!"

To help you in planning dates, we have also included an extensive list of great activities for dates in the Appendix. Check it out, and put it to good use.

Contacting Girls: E-mail vs. Phone Call

E-mail is a great way to initially contact a girl and an easy way to build rapport and gather information about her hobbies and interests. E-mail is also completely acceptable for inviting a girl on a first date. Forget the myths that warn against asking a girl out over e-mail. Our friend Samantha had this to say about guys calling her:

> "I hate talking on the phone with a guy I've just met. He always seems to call at a bad time. We usually have nothing to talk about, and there's always long, awkward pauses of silence. Half the time it takes me a while to remember who he is and where I met him. It just never goes over well.
> But I love e-mailing. When I talk with a guy on the phone, that's my own personal time. But e-mailing I do at work. And I love

taking a break from work to e-mail a guy. It's fun, especially when we shoot a few e-mails back and forth in the same day. This is one thing that all of my friends seem to agree on."

Remember to always be patient. Just because you've met the girl doesn't mean you immediately need to ask her on a date. Casual e-mailing for a week or two is a great way to find out her interests and make her more comfortable around you.

Some girls are so enthusiastic after meeting you that you can ask them out a few days later. With other girls it can take about two or three weeks of e-mail exchanges before the timing seems right. So you will have to feel it out and make sure that a secure level of comfort has been reached before offering an invite. The last thing you want to do is ruin what would otherwise become a great relationship simply because you asked the girl out too soon.

The other great thing about exchanging a few e-mails is that it gives the girl a few chances to mention some great date ideas. You never know when she'll mention:

"A few of my co-workers just came back from the new sushi place down on 2nd St. and raved about it—I wish I had gone with them."

To which you can simply reply:

"Oh, I didn't even know that place was open yet. I love sushi—you want to grab lunch there one day next week?"

Now, don't get us wrong. We don't mean that you should *never* call a girl. What we're saying is when you've only recently met a girl, start things off by e-mailing. At least this will remind her of who you are, and let's be honest, girls can meet quite a few guys in one weekend. Once you've exchanged a few e-mails, a phone call will then go over much more smoothly.

If you have any questions, please e-mail us at menofccr@menofccr.com. Keep in mind that we also offer courses and one-on-one consultations; more information is available at www.menofccr.com.

Chapter 6 – From Dating to a Relationship

Earlier in the book, we said that the first step in dating is making a girl initially attracted to you. The second step is then making a connection with her. So how do you ensure that the two of you connect? To most guys, a connection is a fairly foreign concept. Most male readers are probably thinking, "What the hell is a connection?" A connection is when two people feel that they understand each other because of shared emotions. They intuitively understand what each other is feeling.

How do you connect with someone? Remember the key to compassion: emotion matching. If she's happy, get happy with her. If she's sad, get sad with her. Compassion is really the key to connecting with a woman.

Showing her compassion will allow her to open up to you, and to tell you close and personal things. We've previously talked about using the questions in the Appendix to start a conversation with a girl, and to find out more about her. By continuing this in further conversations, the two of you will naturally gravitate toward more serious topics, such as: her relationship with her family, her past relationships with men, hobbies that she has a passion for, political issues that she feels very strongly about, and religion. All of these are topics about which she will often have very strong feelings. When the conversation gravitates toward these topics, exude compassion.

Listen to her. Show interest in the topic. Show interest in her as a person, and what she has to say. Show interest in how she *feels* about the topic. Make intense eye contact with her. Listen attentively to her. Show her that you really understand her. Show that you really understand what matters most to her. Most importantly, show her that you really understand how she feels about these topics.

A problem that many guys have is that the topics we listed above, the topics leading to a strong connection, are often topics that men want to avoid discussing. For example, if a woman has opposing political viewpoints, or is of a different religion, it is natural to avoid discussing these things in conversation (and wise to avoid when you have first met—recall the section on Reticence). But over time, the continued avoidance of these topics is hindering the connection between the two of you. She will feel as though you don't really know her. In these cases, ask for her viewpoints, and ask how she feels about these issues. Show her that while you may disagree with her, you respect her views and can understand why she feels this way.

So many guys make the mistake of saying something like, "That's so stupid. How can you support that issue?" Sure, you may think it's stupid, but do not express it in that manner. You will be so much better off asking why she supports that issue, and really understanding how she feels about it. Then you can respond with, "That's very interesting. I can see why you are such a huge supporter of this cause and, while

I have an opposing viewpoint, it is very commendable that you have taken a stand. "

Another hot-button topic that most men avoid is letting a woman discuss her past relationships. Understand immediately that discouraging talk on this subject is also a hindrance to making a connection. Women connect by sharing their most intimate feelings, and if there have been other men in her past whom she has felt strongly about (and you know that there have), do not keep her from sharing those feelings with you. In fact, the best way to help a woman let go of past relationships is to encourage her to share her feelings about those relationships with you. Through sharing these feelings, she will connect with you, and her feelings for her ex-boyfriend will rapidly dissipate.

Keep in mind, however, that most girls are taught at a young age not to talk about their ex-boyfriends with a guy they're currently dating. They are taught that guys do not want to hear about their past relationships. It is therefore important to make the girl feel comfortable talking about her past relationships. Encourage her to open up about her past relationships; even ask her questions about these relationships.

Don't be too aggressive, though. You don't want the girl to feel as if you're prying into her past. Show genuine interest in her and her life, and show that this is something that you care about because you care about knowing who she is as a person, and how she became who she is today. This is possibly the most personal topic that a girl can discuss, and this is exactly why discussing past relationships enhances the connection between two people. Our good friend Tara had this to say about the moment that she felt a connection with her current boyfriend Billy:

> "I remember clearly what made me feel so connected to Billy. It was on our first date. We went wine tasting for the day at a nearby vineyard. After tasting quite a few wines, I mentioned how this beautiful day

reminded me of my ex-boyfriend and all the fun we used to have when we went wine tasting.

As soon as I let that slip out, I realized that I never should have said it. In fact, I started apologizing to Billy and said how sorry I was for bringing it up. But, unlike most guys, Billy wasn't the least bit upset. In fact, he started asking questions about my ex-boyfriend, and we spent the next hour talking about him.

From this conversation, Billy could see that I had strong feelings for my ex, as you'd expect when you date someone for almost 3 years. But I think I also showed Billy that I'm ready to move on.

I felt like that discussion about my ex really helped the two of us connect."

So many guys think that connecting with a girl has to do with shared experiences and shared interests, such as both having been to Rome, or both loving to ski. This certainly helps, because you now have common experiences or interests through which to connect. But ultimately sharing the experiences or interests alone is not enough. You have to share how these experiences and interests make you feel.

Now let's look at a complaint that we often hear from guys when we teach CCR in our courses:

"So you mean that I'm supposed to share my feelings with a girl? I'm not sure I really want to do that."

Actually, no. By definition, a connection is when two people feel that they understand each other because of shared emotions. So you would think that this would require both people to open up and share their emotions. Luckily, however, you don't have to do this. Women have become very accustomed to two things:

a) Guys not understanding their (women's) feelings

b) Guys not sharing their own feelings

What we've found is that if you can simply do Part a, you'll be so far ahead of every other guy, that you don't need to worry about doing Part b for now.

Be the guy who understands what a woman is feeling, by showing compassion, matching her emotions, and creating that connection. You do not have to share your own feelings to connect with a woman. In fact, we have found through our experiences that when most guys try to share their own feelings, they are so bad at it that it hurts the relationship more than it helps it.

For example, when men try discussing their past relationships with women, they often end up conveying how little they know about women, instead of showing their feelings. Or when men try talking about political issues, they end up ranting and raving about the issue itself, rather than how the issue makes them feel. The bottom line is this: Stick to Part a for now. And don't worry about attempting to share your own feelings.

Our friend Blair had this to say about a guy she had been dating:

"Marc was a great listener. He really encouraged me to open up about my ex-boyfriend, and I could tell he was interested in what had happened, and how it made me feel. This was amazing, because I've never had a guy show interest in me like this before! I couldn't imagine why a man like this was still single.

But I started to realize why when Marc started talking about his ex-girlfriend. And I could tell from this how little he understands women. He went on and on about how he did a lot of little things for her, such as buying flowers and taking her out to dinner; yet she seemed quite distant to him and eventually ended up dumping him.

He had been working long hours, and sure he occasionally went out to dinner with her, but most nights he came home so late they didn't even get a chance to talk. I could immediately see that Marc didn't understand the importance of spending time with his girlfriend, and really didn't understand women in general."

Now look at what a friend of ours, Niki, had to say about her boyfriend Bryan, who never attempted to share his feelings with her, but certainly understood Niki's feelings:

"I'll never forget the moment I really felt connected with Bryan. One evening, he came over to watch a movie with me, and I just started balling. We hadn't even put the movie in yet. There was no real reason; I think it was mostly a hormonal thing, PMS and stuff.

Anyway, in the past, my boyfriends would've yelled at me, like, 'Why are you crying?' or, 'Jeez, are you PMS-ing?' But Bryan was so calm and compassionate. He just put his arm around me and let me cry on his shoulder. He asked what was wrong, and there was nothing really wrong but I started talking about my job and a conversation I had had with my mom and random stuff.

None of it really mattered. I wasn't really upset about anything; I just needed to cry. Bryan was the first guy who actually *understood* me. He didn't try to solve my problems; it's like he knew there wasn't really a problem, that I just needed to cry. After that night, I really felt connected with Bryan, and we'd only been dating two weeks."

One final word on sharing your feelings in a relationship. In our courses, we inevitably get a follow-up question on this topic:

"You say that guys don't have to share their feelings, at least in the early stages of a relationship. Then why do women always complain that we (men) don't share our feelings?"

Here's what we've found. When women say something like, "Why don't you ever talk about your feelings?" it almost always means, "You don't understand my feelings." If your girlfriend or wife gets upset because you're not sharing your feelings, sit down with her and ask her how she feels. And let her talk it out. We have found, time after time, that women in these instances feel so much better after sitting down and talking about their own feelings. Even if you didn't get a word in edgewise during the entire conversation!

Let's now move on to the games people play in the early stages of a relationship. Here's one word of advice: DON'T. You should never feel hurt if you invite a woman to do something and she doesn't want to do it or can't make it. Remember, you're not her number one priority (at least not yet!). And always remain upbeat if a girl cancels on you. Here's an example of an appropriate response:

Julie: "Jake, I'm really sorry, but I can't come over for dinner tonight. You are so sweet for offering to cook for me, but I completely forgot that it's my neighbor's birthday today."

Jake: "Hey, Julie, no problem. We can definitely reschedule. Wish your neighbor happy birthday for me."

A week and a half later, Jake cooked dinner *and breakfast* for Julie, because he didn't make the mistake of becoming upset with Julie when she backed out of their dinner plans. This is how a confident Man of CCR behaves.

Forget pride. If she doesn't respond to a call or e-mail right away, don't let that stop you from trying to contact her again. It's not a contest. Here's a good example why you should never play pride games:

Dave and Nancy worked for the same company, but never really met before seeing each other at a bar one night. They hit it off really well and Dave got her contact information. They exchanged a few e-mails over the next week, and Nancy asked Dave if he would like to join her and her friends at Millie's Bar. Dave had a softball game that night, but he thought he could still make it, so he told Nancy he would touch base with her so they could meet after his game.

Pumped about getting together, Dave called Nancy's cell phone Tuesday afternoon, but he got her voicemail. He thought that he'd probably hear from her by the end of the day. But by the time Dave's game was over, there was still no word from Nancy. Dave was irritated by Nancy's lack of consideration; he really wanted to go out. Maybe she didn't want to hang out with him after all.

Before making a rash decision, he paused and reflected what a Man of CCR would do. A Man of CCR wouldn't care if a girl didn't call him back, he thought. A Man of CCR doesn't play pride games. So he gave Nancy another call. Nancy answered the phone and sounded excited to hear Dave's voice. She told Dave which bar she was at and he rushed to meet her. It turned out that Nancy had had her phone off most of the day and simply hadn't bothered to check her voicemail. Just think of what Dave would have missed out on if he had played pride games.

Next we get to a crucial point in time: intimacy. Sometimes the first time you kiss is automatic sex. But don't expect it. Often it takes a few dates before this happens. Maintain your patience. Don't suddenly become that aggressive male who needs sex, pressuring a girl into having sex or performing oral sex. Learn to relieve yourself in the bathroom the first couple of times you are with a girl and the payoff will be well worth it. You have come so far already; don't ruin yourself by rushing things. If you try to take it too fast, the girl will think you're interested in her only as a sex object, not as a person. And that's one way to scare a woman off *really* quickly. A friend of ours, Riley, had this to say about her date with Nick:

"I had the most amazing date with Nick. We grabbed lunch at this beautiful café out on the harbor. Then afterward, we rented paddleboats. It was such a great, relaxing time. It was a beautiful day, the sun was shining, the conversation was flowing, and it was so much fun!

We went back to my place after and started kissing on the couch. Nick started kissing me lower and lower. First, my belly button, and then eventually he started kissing me, well, you know. It was amazing! But after that Nick started acting weird, pressuring me to return the favor.

And when I wouldn't, he just sat there sulking.

I'm sorry, but I just don't feel comfortable doing those things on a first date. He made me feel like all he cared about was sex. It's like the whole great day we had together didn't matter because I wouldn't sleep with him. I thought I'd finally met a guy who was interested in me for me, not for sex, but once again I'm wrong. Nick's just like all the others."

Hopefully, she wants you badly enough that on the first hook-up she'll let you give her oral sex. (Of course, if she doesn't want to receive oral sex, don't force her). Go down for a long time. Give her orgasm after orgasm. Don't be selfish. Don't care if she goes down on you or if she has sex with you. Keep making her cum. Spend the night there and give her oral sex again in the morning.

Why do you want to do this? Well, because girls *LOVE* oral sex. This cannot be overstated enough. It is often difficult for many women to have an orgasm the first time they have sex with a new partner because they're uncomfortable or feel guilty about the situation. Additionally, most women do not routinely cum from regular sex. But almost every woman will orgasm from well-performed oral sex.

On your first sexual encounter with a girl, provide her with great oral sex and worry about yourself later in the bathroom if you have to. By doing this, especially if she orgasms, she will want you in her bedroom every night for the rest of her life. Oh, and she'll tell all of her friends about your wizardry as well!

Now let's backtrack a bit. Before you actually sleep with a girl, you should decide ahead of time whether or not you want to date this girl seriously, or if you just want this to be a casual thing. You need to make this decision early because you never know when the topic will come up in conversation.

Suppose 10 minutes after you start kissing, when you're rolling around naked on the living room floor, she says, "Wait, wait. What's going on between the two of us?"

If you haven't already given some thought to what you want to happen between the two of you, then you're in a pretty tight spot (most guys do end up in this situation). You know that you need to tell the girl the truth, but when guys are lying there physically prepared to go, they'll say whatever it takes to have sex—now. This is not a good thing.

Most guys tell a girl what they think she wants to hear just to have sex with her. Such as, "Yeah, I'm interested in a serious relationship." Or "Yes, I love you." The truth is that you can be honest with a girl and she will still sleep with you. So don't make a habit out of lying to a girl just to sleep with her. That's not what a Man of CCR does. And it will only end up hurting her and hurting your chances with other women in the end.

What should you do if you are interested in dating a girl seriously? In this case, just tell her the truth. Tell her that you think she's a great person, and you're definitely interested in dating her seriously. If she shares your interest, you'll sleep together and the two of you can go on to have a great physically and emotionally satisfying relationship.

Now let's take a look at the more complicated case: the case where you are only interested in a casual relationship. Be honest and use the following as a guideline:

> "I'm really not interested in a serious relationship right now."

The key thing here is that you didn't tell her that you're not interested in *dating*. You didn't tell her that all you want is sex. All you did is tell her that you don't want a *serious* relationship. This leaves the decision in the girl's hands. Girls like sex just as much as we do, and although they usually prefer serious relationships, they'll often quite willingly enter into a casual relationship. The most important thing is that you are honest and up front with the woman.

Chapter 7 – The Power of Friendship

Let's back up to the chapter "Getting Started: How to Meet Women" and the importance of meeting women in Naturally-Inviting Environments. We stated that the most natural, inviting way to meet women is through a mutual friend, and that this is how we meet most of the women whom we date. In this chapter, we will take a closer look at the importance of having female friends.

Vouching

Undoubtedly, the best way to meet women is through other female friends. And, the best way to make women want you is to have women talk to other women about you in a way that suggests that they want you. We refer to the positive response a female has toward you, as a result of something she has heard or seen about you from other females, as *Vouching*. There are three types of vouches: the *Direct Vouch*, the *Indirect Vouch*, and the *Subconscious Vouch*.

Direct Vouch

A *Direct Vouch* is a positive statement about you from a female friend of yours to her female friend. Receiving a direct vouch is one of the best ways to befriend new women quickly. When you become a true Man of CCR, you will earn plenty of these.

Our friend, Dave, recalled a direct vouch he received from a female friend:

> Megan: "You've got to come to my party tomorrow night. My friend Susan will be there, and I've told her that she has to meet you. And she's single."
>
> Dave: "I'm going for sure. Your parties are always cool. And if Susan's your friend, she must be fun."
>
> Megan: "And, she's really cute."
>
> Dave: "As long as she's as cool as you are."

Because Susan heard how great a guy Dave was from someone she trusts, automatically she had a favorable impression of him. Dave hit it off with Susan that night, and all he had to do was be himself: a Man of CCR.

Let's take a moment to look at how Dave incorporated several concepts we've already discussed into his short conversation with Megan:

- He responded to Megan with the same enthusiasm about meeting Susan as Megan had for Susan meeting Dave (emotion matching and positive attitude).
- He showed interest in Susan as a person, not a sex object, by implying he wants to meet Susan because she will be cool and fun, rather than wanting to meet her to get down in her pants.

- He re-emphasized that personality is much more of an important quality to him than are looks.

Dave has since had a great relationship with Susan. And yes, she is really cute. Our friend Michelle had this to say about the effect of a vouch:

> "It's really important to me that my friends approve of any guy I'm dating or hooking up with, and I know that if a girlfriend of mine introduces me to a guy that she's friends with, that's her approval right there."

Indirect Vouch

The second type of vouch is the *Indirect Vouch*. This is when a girl sees a guy with one of her female friends. Even though that friend may not expressly vouch for the guy (which would be a direct vouch), the guy is still indirectly vouched for merely by being seen with the girl's female friend.

For example, if Jake walks into Kendra's party and Kendra walks up and gives Jake a big hug, every friend of Kendra's automatically assumes that Jake is a great guy, because Kendra has just indirectly vouched for him. Notice the subtle difference between a direct and indirect vouch. In a direct vouch, Kendra would have explicitly told her friends about Jake. In this indirect vouch, Kendra merely walked up and hugged Jake. Yet both vouches are extremely powerful.

Think about how valuable the indirect vouch is if you go to a bar. If you go with a male friend to a bar to hit on girls, you will have to randomly approach women, and take your chances on whether or not they have a boyfriend or you are bothering them in some other manner.

The majority of times that we go out to a bar, we invite some female friends to come along with us. They will inevitably bring along some of their other friends, and that provides two major advantages over approaching random women. First of all, the bar suddenly turns into a Naturally-Inviting Environment (at least for these women), because we will be introduced by a mutual friend. Above that, we will receive an indirect vouch simply by having this mutual friend. In many cases, it often ends up as a direct vouch, as our female friends were busy telling their friends about us on the way over to the bar.

Subconscious Vouch

The *Subconscious Vouch* is similar to the indirect vouch. This subtle vouch is extremely powerful and is defined as the positive feeling a woman gets by seeing you interact with fun, attractive women whom they don't know (if they knew the women, it would be an indirect vouch). Subconsciously these women think that because these fun, attractive women are spending so much time with you that you must have something to offer.

Here's an example of how the subconscious vouch worked for our student, Dave:

Dave had a good friend, Tracy, who had an out-of-town boyfriend. Tracy would often see her boyfriend on the weekends, but when she didn't, she needed to do things—to stay active and social so she wouldn't miss her boyfriend too much. Tracy is one of the coolest girls we have ever met and, as you will see, provides excellent subconscious vouches.

One weekend last summer Tracy's boyfriend couldn't come visit, so she asked Dave if he had any plans. Dave did have plans. He was going to the beach to visit his friend, Mike, along with several other friends from college. There was a mixed group going, both guys and girls, so it was easy and natural for Dave to invite Tracy along.

When everyone at the beach saw the way Dave and Tracy interacted, they thought the two had been dating forever. Tracy and Dave took shots together. They got in funny poses and took pictures. They danced. They laughed. They chased each other on the beach and in the water.

At one point in the evening a really cute girl, Sharon, started dancing with Dave. It was only the first time Dave had met her. As the two danced, Sharon asked Dave if Tracy would mind him dancing with her. When Dave told her that Tracy wasn't his girlfriend, just a really good friend, Sharon was amazed. She actually told Dave how incredible she thought he was for being able to have such a close relationship with a female friend and not have it turn sexual.

Whenever friends invite us to go out anywhere, from going to a party to grabbing dinner to seeing a baseball game, we almost always each invite a female friend to go with us. Now that we realize the power of the subconscious vouch, we make sure to show up everywhere with a fun, good-looking girl by our side.

The best women to provide subconscious vouches are women either who have out-of-town boyfriends, or whose boyfriends are extremely busy, such as in medical school. The great thing about this symbiotic relationship is that you are each providing the other with a favor. Women who don't get to see their boyfriends much still need to have fun and keep themselves occupied. In return for bringing them along to fun activities, these women will provide you with a great subconscious vouch. The best part about this is that there is no confusion at all about the relationship. You know that she has a boyfriend, and you are fine with it; and she loves the fact that you're the one guy who doesn't mind that she has a boyfriend. We hope that you will no longer make the common mistake of ending a conversation with a girl you've just met simply because she mentions her boyfriend.

We want to re-emphasize the importance of giving compliments, showing compassion, and providing reassurance 100 percent of the time. We have a friend, Deborah, whom we've known for 7 years—long before uncovering CCR. She never once introduced us to one of her female friends. She never once vouched for us. Laurie, on the other hand, is a friend of ours with an out-of-town boyfriend. We've only known Laurie for 2 months, but because we now know CCR, she *LOVES* us. She has introduced us to 6 of her female friends, all fun and attractive, who also love us because of the vouches we received from Laurie.

When you get invited to someone else's event or party, a girl's or a guy's, it might be a *Dudefest.* A dudefest is a party or event with mostly guys and few single women. Men of CCR know how to handle this situation properly.

The most important thing at a dudefest is to stay calm, stay confident, and talk to the other guys. Don't get upset. More than likely you'll want to leave early. When you do, simply go over to whoever invited you, thank them for the invite, and state something along the lines of:

> "I got up really early this morning and just hit a wall..."
>
> "I have to get up early tomorrow morning so I think I'm going to take off."

Be sure when you're showing your gratitude for being invited that it's done with enthusiasm. This will encourage the hosts to invite you to future events that they plan. Observe Dave in the following example:

Laura and Julia invited Dave to grab a drink with them and some of their friends. Dave was pumped because this usually meant that he would meet some new women. When Dave arrived at Buckley's, however, he saw Laura, Julia, and 8 guys. Dave didn't let this bother him. He sat down, introduced himself to the guy sitting next to him and the guy across from him, and struck up a conversation.

After chatting with two guys, Mark and Sam, for a while, Dave politely excused himself:

Dave: "Well, I got up really early this morning and I'm just exhausted. It was really nice to meet you guys. Hopefully we'll get to hang out again."

Sam: "Yeah, nice to meet you, too."

Mark: "Cool. Take it easy."

Dave then walked over to where Laura and Julia were sitting.

Dave: "Hey, Laura. Hey, Julia. Thanks for inviting me, but I got up really early this morning and I'm just wiped. I definitely want to hang out again."

Dave hugged them both and was home by 9:30. There was a message on his machine from Margaret, a woman he'd recently starting hanging out with, wondering if Dave wanted to watch a movie. Dave called her back and went over to her place.

Another point about friendships with females: *Never* ask a female friend to set you up with one of her friends. To a woman, that's pathetic. It implies that you are desperate, insecure and dependent. Your female friends, because they love you so much, will naturally want to introduce you to their single female friends. There's no need to request it.

Recurring Events

Recurring events, such as a co-ed softball team or a weekly wine-tasting group, are events that occur on an ongoing basis: once a week, once every other week, or even once a month. Recurring events with a co-ed group of friends are great because they provide you with an already-planned event. When you meet new girls you can mention it to them without having to deal with the hassle of planning the event. Another benefit is that you know that you will have a solid group of your female friends at each event, ready and waiting to vouch for you. Yet another benefit is that the girls you invite will, in turn, bring along some of their friends so you will meet more women. A final benefit of recurring events is that the guys whom you invite will, in turn, invite you to parties and events that they plan, where you will meet even more women.

Let's take a look at some recurring events that we highly recommend. Forming a co-ed softball team is a great recurring event. First, it's a great topic of conversation when you meet new girls. You can ask a girl if she's interested in playing softball. Girls will typically respond:

"I love playing, but I'm not that good!"

You can respond to this with:

"No problem. We need players and we're not that good. We don't take it seriously. It's just for fun. Come out and play with us."

Softball will also help you to meet more girls because girls will inevitably bring one of their friends along to play as well. Furthermore, you can generate additional interactions with these girls. For example, if a girl hasn't played softball in a while, you can suggest that the two of you go to a batting cage. You can also suggest that the two of you get together one day after work to throw a ball around. Wine tasting is also a great recurring event. Girls *love* trying new wines. Unlike softball, you won't have any problem getting girls to attend. Guys will gladly attend as well, knowing that there will be a lot of girls there. Wine tasting will also help you meet more girls because, even more so than softball, girls will bring along their female friends. You can also build in extra activities, like an occasional visit to a vineyard on a Saturday.

A varying-activity night is also a good recurring event. This is good because you get to plan a variety of different activities, but you won't get the same group of people every week. This is also a great opportunity to invite a girl you've recently met, because there's sure to be an upcoming activity that she's interested in. Pick a night of the week, and alternate activities every week.

Here's an example of how easily a recurring event allows you to invite and get contact information from a girl that you have just met. Dave met Lisa at their mutual friend Sarah's party. After talking for a few minutes he easily got her contact information and convinced her to participate in his weekly wine tasting:

> Dave: "So I take it you like wine? A few friends and I get together every week and taste a different type of wine. It's a lot of fun. I've learned a lot about wine since we started."
>
> Lisa: "That sounds really cool. Yeah, I would love to come. In fact, I have a friend who I know would like to come, too. Do you mind if I bring her along?"
>
> Dave: "Of course not. The more the merrier. I'll tell you what, give me your e-mail address and when I get into work on Monday I'll

send you the details. Oh, I almost forgot to tell you that Sarah will be there, so you'll know a few people."

For more recurring event ideas, see the Appendix.

Chapter 8 – CCR in Your Career

We wanted to impart the fact that we believe CCR to be more than just a method to meet, approach, and date women. CCR is a way of life. More definitively, CCR is a way to improve all the relationships in your life. We are developing this topic in greater detail for a future book, and wanted to touch upon it now.

Both readers and students have asked us for advice on how to incorporate CCR in the workplace. No, not to pick up women, but to better interact with their peers, managers, and subordinates. After writing this chapter, we asked the Vice President of a Fortune 500 company that one of us used to work for to offer us his critique. This is what he had to say:

> "CCR is really just a general principle of human interaction that should be applied universally. In fact, a lot of your principles overlap with the principles of many of the great leadership gurus, such as John Maxwell. It's humorous that principles the two of you developed for the purpose of enhancing your dating lives are actually

fundamental leadership and management principles. It's humorous, but not surprising. After all, the goals are the same—to develop a relationship that will grow into a successful alliance. I completely agree with everything you've written."

With this said, let's take a brief look at how to apply CCR in the workplace.

Building employee morale. Something that the great leadership gurus preach is to provide both private and public recognition of your employees' accomplishments. This is just the workplace version of ensuring that you provide women with plenty of compliments. We discussed complimenting women on physical and personal characteristics when you first meet, and then moving toward more meaningful compliments as your relationship progresses. As a manager, be sure to compliment your employees on both their work and behavioral characteristics that help them succeed. For example, a simple, yet effective, compliment is:

> "Thanks for getting that report to me a day early. I really appreciate your punctuality, and just want you to know that it's really great having someone as dependable as you when it comes to meeting deadlines."

This simple compliment, said sincerely, can make an employee's day! It will also serve to reinforce your employee's positive behavior, and ensure that he/she knows the importance of this dependability.

Earning the respect and trust of your peers, subordinates, and managers. Too many people don't make the proper attempt to build respect and trust among their co-workers, the people whom they spend the most time around on a daily basis. Ask questions about your co-workers' lives, and show genuine, sincere interest in them as people. Of course, don't pry. Some people don't want to bring their personal lives into the workplace, but they are in the rare minority. We were very successful with getting our co-workers to open up to us about who they're dating, their kids, their families, anything that mattered to them. Most people love talking about themselves and their personal lives, so encourage it.

By building a trusting connection with your peers, subordinates, and managers, they will all feel comfortable coming to you with personal matters and with confidential, work-related matter.

Providing constructive criticism / Motivating employees. Often you will have to provide your employees, or peers, with constructive criticism. Actually, you should probably do this more often than you do, but if you're like most people you avoid it at all costs. You wait until the employee's review period, and put the feedback on his or her review, which isn't fair because you haven't provided them with the opportunity to improve prior to their review. And the review is often what determines the size of their raise or the amount of their incentive.

We have found that sometimes people just need a little bit of reassurance, someone to believe in them. By reassuring someone that they *can* do the job, and offering to work with them to improve, you can really motivate someone to want to improve. Our friend Ron had this to say about his problems giving presentations:

"I've always been a bad public speaker, and I HATE giving presentations. I just dread them. At least, that was before Michael was my manager. Previous managers had sent me to training, and tried other techniques to improve my public-speaking skills.

But Michael did something that no one else had done before: he simply reassured me that my next presentation would be great. He showed a belief in me that no one had before, and by reassuring me that everything would be OK, it gave me confidence. And my next presentation was great!

For the first time I was confident in front of a room of people. Sure, I was still nervous, but Michael was sitting in the front row nodding his head in reassurance as I went through the material. It's amazing that after everything my previous managers had tried, it was this simple step that provided the greatest results."

Leading a team. From our experience in Corporate America, the overwhelming majority of people do not like their managers. Imagine being one of the few managers whom people like. By being a Man of CCR, and by being confident, upbeat, and enthusiastic, people will *want* to work for you. We conducted a study about a year ago where one of us was employed at the time. We made a list of the most well-liked and admired managers in the department. And believe it or not, every single one of them embodied the characteristics of a Man of CCR (quite a few were actually Women of CCR). It was at this point that we realized the broad application of this material.

If you are a Man of CCR at work, not only will people want to work for you, but they'll also put their best foot forward for you. Retention will be high, and your employees will tell their friends in other parts of the company who are whining and complaining about their managers, how much they love working for *you*. Other employees in the company will even request transfers to your team. And that's going to reflect well on your career.

Giving presentations. A lot of the material we have presented in this book applies broadly to communications. One specific area in which to apply this material is when giving presentations. For instance, the importance of eye contact when speaking is greatly understated. Observe most people giving presentations. They either stare off into space, or they glance nervously around the room.

The proper way to speak to a room of people is to make eye contact with each person in the room for two or three seconds at a time. By doing this, you will draw your listeners into the topic, as each person in the room will think that you are speaking directly to them. Observe the greatest speakers; you'll see that this is in fact their technique.

Presenting a controversial / conflicting viewpoint. Presenting a dissenting opinion is not difficult to do, and can be valuable to a team; yet most people are afraid to speak up, probably because they don't know how to adequately express a conflicting viewpoint. One of the most important behaviors when entering into a hostile discussion is to be respectful of others' opinions and viewpoints. Ask questions and listen to what they have to say. Pay attention when they're speaking, and show genuine interest in what others have to say.

One of our former co-workers, Renee, had this to say about Jon, another co-worker who is highly respected for his ability to coerce others:

> "One thing that I notice about Jon, unlike most people, is that when he's expressing his point-of-view, he doesn't make you feel stupid. He always respects what you have to say, and merely offers his point-of-view as an alternate solution. He makes you feel respected while simultaneously

convincing you that his suggestion might actually be the better way to go."

Managing change. Change is inevitable in any organization. Change causes a lot of questions and low morale among employees, because most managers do a poor job of communicating the changes to their employees and they provide little reassurance. Reassure your employees that everything will be OK. Encourage them to come to you with questions.

And you should ask questions, too. Find out what your employees' main concerns and fears are. Is it layoffs? Do they think that their promotion is in jeopardy? Reassure them that you will stick up for them and ensure that they are treated fairly. Of course, all this is moot if you don't follow through on your promises.

Laying off an employee. While almost no one enjoys this activity, there is a proper way to approach the activity. The use of compassion will make him/her feel better when dealing with what will undoubtedly be a tough time. Instead of coldly saying:

> "Yeah, you know, we're going through really tough times right now. And I didn't want to do it, but I didn't have a choice. It was a mandate from above."

Try something along the lines of:

> "I realize this is very difficult news for you to take, and I wish that circumstances were different. You've made a lot of important contributions to the company, but unfortunately, as a company, we're not doing well right now. We've had some difficult decisions to make, and unfortunately this is one of them."

Helping a team member through problems. Often a member of your team will need support, either with work-related problems or personal problems. When this time comes, turn to CCR. Ask your team member questions to show him/her that you genuinely care. Show interest in this employee as a person, and be sincere in this interest. This will encourage both this team member, and other members of your team, to trust you with their problems, which is an important component to being seen as a leader.

Building support for an initiative. Often in your career you will have to build support for an initiative, either within your own team or on another team. When doing this, it is important how you convey your own support for this initiative. Be positive, upbeat, and enthusiastic, and this will convey to others that you really believe in the initiative. Only if others really believe that you support this initiative will they be swayed to support it as well.

Many of you probably use many aspects of CCR in your daily lives right now. But what we've tried to do with this book is allow you to pinpoint what you're NOT doing. Recognizing the aspects of CCR that are missing from your routine will, as illustrated in this chapter, also help improve your effectiveness at work. Because CCR is not only a way to improve your relationships with women, but it is also a method for improving your relationships at work as well.

Chapter 9 – Coping with Life as a Man of CCR

Once you become a Man of CCR, your life will change. For the most part, these changes are positive and extreme, but there are also times when being a Man of CCR is difficult and not exactly the way that you fantasized it would be. This chapter will enlighten you to some of the challenges you will face.

Challenge #1: *Handling the ease with which you now approach women.* It will be odd at first, but you will no longer be nervous when approaching a woman. You will be calm and confident, because you know exactly what to do.

Challenge #2: *Dealing with actually having something to talk about when you meet a woman.* This too will take a little getting used to, but you will actually have great conversations with women. No more awkward silences, and no more panicking about what to say next, just relaxed, flowing conversation.

Challenge #3: *Accepting that a lot of women will want to give you their contact info.* This is a side effect of the previous challenge. Now that you have great conversation with women, it will no longer be awkward to ask for contact information. In fact, women will quite willingly provide this to you, and it will actually be their correct info! Accepting that women now want you to contact them is a welcome challenge as a Man of CCR.

Challenge #4: *Becoming accustomed to frequent dates that are relaxing and enjoyable.* You will no longer have to deal with uncomfortable first dates, where each of you is wondering what to do or say next. Your dates will be so natural and relaxed that you won't even think of them as dates because dates are supposed to be stressful, and this is just too easy.

Challenge #5: *Getting used to a tremendous sex life.* With success in meeting women, talking to them, getting their contact info, and having relaxing dates comes, of course, a lot of sex. After years of being pathetic, this is something that we just weren't prepared for. After all, sex is tiring; some days we just walk around as zombies. Having all of this sex and still finding the energy to live the rest of your life will be a tremendous challenge.

Challenge #6: *Adjusting to relationships that are fulfilling and successful.* We know, we know, relationships aren't *supposed* to work out. But imagine how great it is when they actually do. When you actually understand the person you are dating, and can properly relate to her. As a Man of CCR, you will end up in successful, fulfilling relationships that will make all of your friends in dead-end relationships jealous.

It can be tough dealing with the challenges that come from living life as a Man of CCR, but the sacrifices are well worth it. When those other guys come around asking why every girl loves you and how you have so many dates and can approach women with ease, we'd appreciate it if you'd tell them about this book. There's an order form inside the back cover.

And if you ever have any questions about CCR, please e-mail us at menofccr@menofccr.com. We'll be more than happy to help out. We also offer courses (currently in New York City and San Francisco) and one-on-one consultations over the phone; check www.menofccr.com for details. Thanks for reading, and congratulations. You're on your way to being a Man of CCR!

AFTERWORD

Becoming a Man of CCR is incredible! When you sincerely compliment girls, show them compassion, and provide reassurance, they will really enjoy being around you. Approach women with great conversation and a confident, positive attitude and they will *want* to give you their contact info. Invite women to do things that you know interest them, and focus on the conversation, and women will LOVE being around you because of how good you make them feel. And they'll be so impressed that you're interested in them as a person, *not* as a sex object, that they'll *want* to sleep with you, as they did with us and with the many others we've taught CCR to. Finally, you'll end up in strong relationships, because you understand exactly what women are looking for.

The next step is up to you. CCR is extremely powerful, so go ahead and start using it. Refer back to this book when you have questions, or shoot us an e-mail (menofccr@menofccr.com). Tell us your stories. Tell us all about the great girl you met by using the techniques in this book, and how she *gave* you her contact info without you even asking. We'll put the best stories on our web site!

Good luck,

John Fate & Steve Reil

Glossary

Bothersome Environments – One of three types of environments in which to meet women (the other two are Naturally-Inviting Environments and Moderately-Inviting Environments). Bothersome environments are the toughest environments in which to meet women, because you are interrupting them from some other activity. Unfortunately, bothersome environments are also the most common places to meet women. These include: bars, bookstores, concerts, subways, buses, restaurants, coffee shops, grocery stores, festivals, parks, and walking down the street.

CCR – It is the premise of this book. It is an acronym that stands for Compliments, Compassion, and Reassurance. By sincerely complimenting women, showing them compassion, and reassuring them that things will be ok in times of need, you make women feel good about themselves. This makes women want to be around you. When combined with a positive, confident attitude, women will *WANT* you.

Category 1 Guy – One of the three categories of guys who traditionally got women. Category 1 guys are really good-looking.

Category 2 Guy – One of the three categories of guys who traditionally got women. Category 2 guys are rich.

Category 3 Guy – One of the three categories of guys who traditionally got women. Category 3 guys are famous (including local celebrities).

Category 4 Guy – The new category of guys who get women: Men of CCR.

Direct Vouch – A positive statement about you from a female friend of yours to a female friend of hers. An example is, "Jen, you have to meet my friend Dave!! He is really awesome!!" Receiving *direct vouches* is one of the best ways to befriend new women quickly. As you develop into a Man of CCR, you will receive more and more of these.

Dudefest – You know what this is! It's when you end up at a party or event with mostly guys and few single women. Men of CCR know how to handle this annoying situation properly.

Emotion Matching – This is the key to compassion. By matching a woman's mood, whether it is happy or sad, she feels connected to you emotionally.

Golden Rule of CCR – If you don't have anything CCR to say, don't say anything at all!

Indirect Vouch – This vouch occurs when you and the girl you've just met have a close mutual female friend. This girl that you've just met will be much more receptive toward you knowing that you are good friends with a friend of hers.

Man of CCR – This is what you become once you've read and implemented what we suggest in this book. This man compliments women, shows compassion toward them, and reassures them. He projects a positive, confident attitude toward women. As a result, women love this type of guy. This, in turn, makes even more women want him. Women want a Man of CCR as much as one who is rich, famous, or really good-looking!

Moderately-Inviting Environments – One of three types of environments in which to meet women (the other two are Naturally-Inviting Environments and Bothersome Environments). Moderately-inviting environments are, as the name might suggest, moderately easy places to meet women. Some examples include: a co-ed sports team, a wine-tasting class, the local chapter of your alumni association, and a church or temple. When women are in these environments, their primary purpose often isn't to meet new people. They are usually, however, aware that they will meet new people through these groups and clubs, and thus are moderately inviting toward men who may approach them.

Naturally-Inviting Environments – One of three types of environments in which to meet women (the other two are Moderately-Inviting Environments and Bothersome Environments). Naturally-Inviting environments are the easiest environments in which to meet women, such as at a party where a mutual friend is likely to introduce you.

Relinquishing Short-Term Sexual Desire – Conveying an attitude toward women that you are interested in them as a person, *not* as a sex object.

Subconscious Vouch – This subtle vouch is extremely powerful. This vouch occurs when you bring a fun, attractive female friend to an event with you, and other women there see you with her. Subconsciously these other women think you get along well with all women. They will naturally desire you more because they see other fun, attractive women who also enjoy your company.

Third-Party Compliment – A compliment you say to one person regarding someone who is not present. It is the complete opposite of talking badly behind someone's back. It is such a great feeling the first time a female says, "You know, you never have a bad thing to say about anyone. I love the fact that you are always so positive. It's truly refreshing to be around someone who always sees the good in people."

Vouch – The positive response a female has toward you as a result of something positive she has seen or heard about you from other females. There are three types of vouches—the direct vouch, the indirect vouch, and the subconscious vouch.

Appendix A – Questions to Ask a Woman That You Have Just Met

Here are some topics for discussion as you're getting to know a girl. These will allow you to make great conversation, and provide you with ideas for things to invite her to. Do not *ever* ask these questions rapid-fire. These are simply meant to spark conversation, not to be asked sequentially. Inevitably, a question will send the two of you off on some random tangent, allowing you to learn exciting things about her that you never would have thought to ask. That is exactly the purpose of these questions. If you find yourself going through this list in order, then this girl probably doesn't want to talk to you right now. Go talk to someone else.

Background
- So are you from <this city>?
- Oh, where are you originally from?
- Do you like <city you're from>?

- Have you lived there your whole life?
- Where else have you lived?

Current City

- So why'd you come to <this city>?
- How long have you lived here?
- What part of town do you live in?
- What part of town do you normally go out in?
- How often do you go out? (Politely)

Career / Job

- So where do you work?
- Do you like it?
- How long have you worked there?
- Where did you work before that?

School

- So did you go to school around here?
- Where did you go to school?
- Why did you choose <school>?
- Did you like it?
- What did you major in?
- Why did you choose <major>?
- Did you like it?
- Have you thought about going back to school?
- To study what?
- Where have you thought about applying?

Friends

- So, do you have a lot of friends from school who live here in <city>?
- Where did most of your friends end up moving?

- (Try to lead into discussion of cities you've visited or where your friends live)

Family

- So does your family live in <city>?
- Do you visit them often?
- Do you have any siblings?
- Younger or older?
- Where do they live?
- Are you close to them?
    - (Discuss your own siblings, their ages, where they live, and how close you are)

Travel

- Ask if she's been to any cool nearby places, such as a nearby beach, ski resort, National Park, campground, city, tourist attraction, college, vineyard, or lake. Try to get a feel for what she enjoys doing and where she hasn't yet been but would love to go.

Sports

- So did you go to football/basketball games at <school>?
- Are you a sports fan?
- What sports do you follow (if any)?
- Do you play any sports?

Entertainment

- What's your favorite TV show?
- What TV shows do you watch regularly?
- Have you seen any good movies lately?

- What are your favorite types of movies?
- What is your all-time favorite movie?
- Are there any movies out now that you want to see? (Try to be subtle; don't imply too much)

Appendix B – Date Ideas

Here are some ideas for dates, or just fun things to do with a group of mixed-sex friends.

Nature

- Boating
- Fishing
- Canoeing
- Lake
- Hiking
- Camping
- Scenic drive
- Beach
- Skiing / snow boarding
- Tubing
- Caverns
- Jet ski
- Water ski
- Biking
- Picnic

- Roller-blading / Roller-skating
- Walk a girl's dog in a park
- Fly a kite in a park
- Paddle boating
- Barbecue at a friend's pool (or apartment complex's pool)
- Botanical Garden
- Park or other nice outdoor spot
- Walk around nearby college campus
- Apple picking

Culture

- Museum
- Aquarium
- Zoo
- Vineyard
- Play / musical
- Other cultural spots (check local guidebooks)

Amusement / Entertainment

- Theme park
- Movie theater
- Rent a movie
- Miniature golf
- Bowling
- Shoot pool
- Comedy club
- Ice skating
- Water park
- Concert
- Drive-in movie
- Karaoke
- Murder mystery dinner
- Watch horse racing
- Watch polo match

Play sports

- Volleyball
- Tennis (become doubles partners)
- Driving range
- Batting cage
- Racquetball

Sporting Events

- Pro, college, or minor league

Seasonal

- Outdoor concerts in the summertime
- Horse races in the spring/summer
- Halloween
  - Hayride
  - Pumpkin picking
- Christmas
  - Watch the Nutcracker
  - See Christmas lights

Food / Drinks

- Grab lunch during the week
- Sunday brunch
- Grab a drink after work
- Ice cream
- Sushi
- Pastry shop
- Coffee shop
- Grab dessert
- Cook for a girl (***Girls love this!)

- Cook with a girl, or ask her to show you how to make a recipe. (You should at least be minimally capable in the kitchen to request this)
- Order Chinese food or a pizza

Shopping

- Local mall
- Popular shopping district (may be out of town)

Appendix C – Recurring Event Ideas

Softball

Here are some guidelines for building a softball team:

- Join a local city or county league; it should be quite inexpensive.
- Make sure you enter a co-ed, non-competitive league. Do not make the mistake of entering a competitive league. This will scare off and annoy the girls.
- You may have a choice of season length; try to keep the season to about 2 months. Games will probably be weekly.
- Roster size is usually 20-25 people; 10 players usually play at once.
- Invite 7 or 8 guys to join the team; save the rest of the roster spots for girls. Try not to invite any highly competitive guys. This will really annoy the women.

- Go to the batting cage as a team or call a team practice before the season; this will be a good excuse to get all of the girls together.
- Send out a weekly e-mail the day of a game, reminding everyone of the game time, location, and directions. Ask people to respond if they will attend. Include your cell phone number in the e-mail; inevitably someone will get lost or forget the directions.
- You won't have a problem getting guys to attend; if you ever fall short, you can easily find a male friend to play for the day (guys love softball and guys love women—what guy wouldn't join in?)
- You will have problems getting girls to attend. You will probably need to call around each week just to convince 5 girls to show up.
- This used to frustrate us, until we started using it to our benefit. We would purposely try to fall a girl or two short each week so that we could invite a girl we'd recently met to play for the day.
- Do *not* take winning seriously. It is quite possible that you will be really bad. The girls don't mind losing. What girls do mind are highly competitive guys. Don't be that guy. Once again, try not to invite any highly competitive guys to play.
- Consider drinking during the games. This probably won't be permitted, since you'll be playing in a city/county park or on school grounds. Mix something up in a cooler and sneak it in. If anyone asks, just say it's juice.
- The best drink is something sweet with a lot of sugar. We recommend mixing 1-½ gallons of fruit punch with a handle of vodka and a 7-lb. bag of ice. Beer or non-sweet mixed drinks will dehydrate everyone.
- Don't forget to bring the equipment (bats and balls) to each game, or appoint someone to be responsible for it. If you're drinking, bring 25 paper or plastic cups each week.

- Appoint someone on the team to coach. Choose someone who knows softball well, but isn't highly competitive. This will relieve you of the responsibility of keeping track of who hasn't played yet, and listening to people (girls) whine about what position you've stuck them in.
- Have fun with it! It's a bit of work, but in the end it's a lot of fun and of great benefit to you!

Wine-tasting

Here are some guidelines for organizing wine tastings:

- Gather a small group of friends (maybe 10 people) who all know each other.
- Get together once a week or once every other week.
- Taste a new type of wine each week. (Some popular reds are Cabernet Sauvignon, Merlot, Shiraz, Pinot Noir, and Chianti; some popular whites are Chardonnay, Sauvignon Blanc, Pinot Grigio, and Riesling)
- Have a different person host it each week; rotate through the group so that everyone hosts once.
- Each week, have everyone bring a bottle of the chosen grape. It's actually better to state that there should be 1 bottle for every 2 people (any more than this is too much wine). Don't state 1 bottle per couple; this will dissuade single girls from attending.
- With the "1 bottle for every 2 people" rule in place, this makes it easy to call up a girl you've recently met and ask if she'd like to join you for the evening. Tell her you'll get the wine. If things go well, you can suggest that she get the wine next week.
- As people arrive, have the host put each bottle in a brown bag. Write a number on the outside of each bag. Give everyone a wine glass and have everyone rate each wine by number. At the end, remove the brown bags and let people see which wines they

liked best. Then let your friends drink from whichever bottle they please the rest of the evening.
- The host may wish to request that people bring their own wine glasses.
- It is a nice touch for the host to serve appetizers. Cheese and crackers are always popular with wine.
- Send out a weekly e-mail reminding everyone of the host, location, directions, grape, and time. Build enthusiasm by stating how much fun it will be!
- Run the wine-tasting events for 10-12 weeks, and then move on to another activity.
- Wine tasting is a lot of fun. The group size will probably grow each week.

Activity Night

A varying-activity night, in which you get together the same night every week but for a different activity, is also a lot of fun. Here are some good activities to try:

- Ice skating
- Night skiing
- Movie rental
- Bowling
- Potluck dinner
- Pool tournament
- Bar night
- Board/card game
- Miniature golf
- Wine and cheesecake night

Other Recurring Events

Here are some more ideas for recurring events. If you come up with any more, please e-mail us and let us know:

- Get everyone to take a weekly cooking class together
- Get everyone to take a weekly dancing class together (girls love this)
- Have a monthly potluck dinner; host every month or rotate hosts
- Movie night
- Have everyone gather one night a week to watch the popular TV shows
- Plan around actual events, such as a weekly concert series

References

1 – Prevalence, Incidence and Consequences of Violence Against Women Survey, National Institute of Justice and Centers for Disease Control and Prevention, November 2000.

2 – Annie E. Casey Foundation. (1998). Kids Count Special Report: When Teens Have Sex: Issues and Trends. Baltimore, MD: Annie E. Casey Foundation.

3 – AGI – Alan Guttmacher Institute. (1994). Sex and America's Teenagers. New York: Alan Guttmacher Institute.

4 – ANAD Ten Year Study [ANAD is National Association of Anorexia Nervosa & Associated Disorders, anad.org]

5 – American Psychiatric Association Work Group on Eating Disorders. Practice guideline for the treatment of patients with eating disorders (revision). *American Journal of Psychiatry*, 2000; 157(1 Suppl): 1-39.

Quick Order Form

Web Orders: www.menofccr.com
E-mail Orders: sales@menofccr.com
Fax Orders: 775-256-7309
Telephone Orders: see www.menofccr.com
Mail Orders: see www.menofccr.com

Name: _____

Address: _____

City: _____ State: _____ Zip: _____

Telephone: _____

E-mail Address: _____

Shipping & Handling: $2.95/book for all orders in U.S.
(total is $17.90/book in U.S., except in Virginia)

Sales tax: Please add 4.5% for products shipped to
Virginia (total is $18.57/book in Virginia)

Quantity: _____   **Total: $**_____
I understand that I may return any products for a full
refund—for any reason, no questions asked.

Payment: ____check   ____ credit card:
Payment must accompany orders. Allow 3 weeks for
delivery.

____Visa   ____MasterCard

Card number: _____

Name on card: _____Exp. Date: _____

Signature: _____